THE ENGLISH ANCESTRY
AND HOMES OF THE
PILGRIM FATHERS

Will of William Mullins

THE ENGLISH ANCESTRY

AND HOMES

OF THE

PILGRIM FATHERS

WHO CAME TO PLYMOUTH ON THE *MAYFLOWER* IN 1620, THE *FORTUNE* IN 1621, AND THE *ANNE* AND THE *LITTLE JAMES* IN 1623

CHARLES EDWARD BANKS

HERITAGE BOOKS
2009

HERITAGE BOOKS
AN IMPRINT OF HERITAGE BOOKS, INC.

Books, CDs, and more—Worldwide

For our listing of thousands of titles see our website
at
www.HeritageBooks.com

A Facsimile Reprint
Published 2009 by
HERITAGE BOOKS, INC.
Publishing Division
100 Railroad Ave. #104
Westminster, Maryland 21157

Originally published:
New York
1929

— Publisher's Notice —

In reprints such as this, it is often not possible to remove blemishes from the original. We feel the contents of this book warrant its reissue despite these blemishes and hope you will agree and read it with pleasure.

International Standard Book Numbers
Paperbound: 978-0-7884-2021-4
Clothbound: 978-0-7884-8090-4

THE HISTORICAL EVIDENCES

FOREWORD

THE origin and family connections of the Plymouth Pilgrims were apparently of little concern to themselves in the age in which they lived or to their immediate descendants for several generations, for with a few exceptions the contemporary historians of Plymouth Colony—Bradford, Morton and Winslow—made no record of their origin or family associations. Two centuries elapsed before any interest in this subject was manifested, but from the time of the Bicentennial of the landing of the Pilgrims which stimulated a desire to know something of the identity of these pioneers and the recent celebration of the Tercentenary this natural desire was crystallized.

The Dexters, father and son, who made a dozen visits to Leyden to study the lives and origins of the Pilgrims, being themselves descendants of those historic figures, ready to honor, but unwilling to flatter, presented a true picture of their social standing. The city records of Leyden disclosed to these tireless investigators that to secure a livelihood the members of Robinson's church were engaged in over fifty different occupations of manual labor which they enumerated. And the younger Dexter wrote:

"That they engaged in such humble employments as some of these was due to three facts: that many of them had been of lowly station in England; that most of them having been farmers now had to turn to such trades as could be learned easily, and that in most cases having been compelled to sacrifice much of whatever property they had in order to escape from England at all, they were poor and were obliged to accept at once whatever work could be found. . . ."

To approach this subject with an open mind it must be understood at the outset that the Pilgrims were not, with one probable exception, persons of recognized social station in English life of that period. Class distinctions were then well defined and the term "gentleman" had a legal, and not an ethical or cultural significance, as we now apply it. The Pilgrims were of the yeoman class and came from the cottages, not from the manor houses of England. Indeed the large majority were from the tenements of cities and attempts which have been undertaken to make some of them masquerade as scions of the nobility or gentry of England, (*New Light on the Pilgrim Story*), is a distinct disservice to these plain sons and daughters of the field and the loom. It is disproved wherever it has been possible to obtain the true facts respecting their origins.

In the following pages, the Author has not undertaken to emphasize facts in disparagement of their stations in life, nor to claim unwarranted prominence for them, but to present the simple facts in each case, to show as far as is possible their former estate in England to the fullest extent that the scanty references to them permit. Realizing that little could be gleaned from the fields where the Dexters had already labored, the Author devoted about four years to the English records in an attempt to supplement what had been disclosed by the Dexters in the form of clues to the former homes of the Leyden band. It will be noted, however, that the large majority of the "Passengers" of the first four ships never lived in Leyden at all and that most of them came from the great city of London where they had lived in its vast network of lanes and alleys.

CONTENTS

	PAGE
THE HISTORICAL EVIDENCES	1
I. PILGRIM SOURCES IN ENGLAND	1
II. CHILDREN OF THE *Mayflower*	5
III. UNLISTED *Mayflower* PASSENGERS	7
IV. LONDON AS A PILGRIM CENTRE	11
V. STORY OF THE *Mayflower*	17
PASSENGERS OF THE *Mayflower*	25
PASSENGERS OF THE *Fortune*	103
PASSENGERS OF THE *Anne*	135
PASSENGERS OF THE *Little James*	169
FEMALE PASSENGERS	177
INDEXES	181

THE HISTORICAL EVIDENCES

I

PILGRIM SOURCES IN ENGLAND

THE last definite attempt to locate the English origin of that group of Separatists and Brownists, usually designated as the Pilgrims, who left their native land and settled in Amsterdam and Leyden between 1600 and 1620, was made over twenty years ago by the late Henry Martin Dexter and his son, Morton. Their gleanings from the Amsterdam and Leyden archives resulted in the accumulation of a large amount of official information concerning these English exiles, furnishing clues to their former residence, their marriages and existing relationships to each other. These gleanings covered over a hundred family names of persons identified as of membership in the church of which John Robinson was pastor. As only thirty-five of this ascertained membership are identified as coming in the *Mayflower* it will be seen that only a portion of Dexter's information respecting these people is of genealogical interest to descendants in this country.

The Pilgrim Colony in Leyden, definitely known as such, numbered 298 persons, while the English Colony in that city numbered 626 persons. Only seven of the Robinson church members became citizens of Leyden prior to the *Mayflower* emigration. Only a dozen in this colony can be definitely assigned to the Scrooby region whence Robinson, Brewster and Bradford migrated. Of the thirty-five persons—adults and children—who came over in 1620, Dexter gives clues to former residence in only three instances which, added to the three already known (Bradford, Brewster and Winslow), shows the paucity of information obtained by him after years of research.

Only three persons of the Leyden church membership came in the *Fortune* in 1621, but in 1623 twenty-four associated with the Leyden church of Robinson as wives or children of those who had preceded them in the *Mayflower* and *Fortune*, came in the *Anne* and *Little James*. The Leyden records as analyzed by Dexter concerning the origin of the Pilgrims in whom we are interested located their homes in England by the following table:

From the North of England....	Durham	1
	Scotland	3
		— 4
From the East of England.....	Yorks (East)	5
	Norfolk	32
	Suffolk	3
	Essex	11
	Kent	17
		— 68
From the Middle of England...	Yorks (remainder)..	6
	Lincoln	2
	Notts	9
	Cambridge	3
	Leicester	1
	Berkshire	2
	Wiltshire	1
		— 24

From the South of England.... Somerset	5	
Dorset	1	
Sussex	3	
Hampshire	1	
	—	10
From London	17	
	—	17
Uncertain; probably .... Notts, Norfolk, Suffolk or Kent	14	
	—	14
		137

This meagre result, which represented the exhaustive search of the Dexters in Holland, and has not been added to by subsequent investigators, is explained by the now understood and accepted fact that this religious insurrection in England had its principal support from individuals of the yeoman and working classes in widely separated localities whose religious associations were conducted in secret. Many of them were young, unmarried persons who, of course, left no family records behind and who did not enter into the family relation until after reaching Leyden.

The city records of Leyden show that forty-five marriages of Englishmen took place there between 1609–1620. Only nine men who came on the *Mayflower* were married, and from the genealogical standpoint it will thus be seen that identification of these persons in England prior to their removal to Leyden is of extraordinary difficulty. Of the thirty-five men who came on the *Fortune* but eight are known to have been married. With the exception of Brewster and Carver, the Pilgrims who went to Leyden with Robinson were all young people or in early middle life. Bradford had not reached his majority when the Pilgrims went to Holland. The oldest members, as far as ages can be established, were Allerton, Brewster, Carver, Cook and Tilley. Most of those who came in the *Fortune* were "lusty yonge men." Such people left no record behind in the marriage registers of England.

II

CHILDREN OF THE *MAYFLOWER*

SEVEN minors came on the *Mayflower* who were not children of any of the passengers and only one was described as having kinship to any of them. This raises an interesting and important question. In 1617 the Lord Mayor and Aldermen of London "fearing lest the overflowing multitude of inhabitants should, like too much blood, infect the whole city with plague and poverty," devised a remedy for this condition by transporting to the new English settlements in America such children as were without home associations. In 1618, one hundred children were sent to Virginia and in 1619 another shipment of a hundred were sent on request of the Virginia Company. It is not improbable that several of these children, unrelated to any *Mayflower* family, were "transported" at the suggestion of Thomas Weston and there is reasonable evidence that such was the case; but in this instance the children were assigned to the care of specified individuals who accepted them in the relationship of servants or wards. Every parish in London was required to make a contribution annually towards the expense of transporting these waifs. Only two of these children survived to adult years, or remained in Plymouth and became heads of families.

III

MAYFLOWER "PASSENGERS" NOT MENTIONED BY BRADFORD

TO the many who have regarded Bradford as the infallible authority on the names of persons who came to Plymouth in 1620 in the *Mayflower*, it will be somewhat of a surprise to learn that two names should be added to the list. The Mayflower Society includes under the name of "passengers," two ordinary seamen who were employed to remain as servants of the Colony in such employment as would be required of them in the fisheries for a definite term. In like manner John Alden was employed as a cooper to look after the hogsheads of beer on the voyage to prevent loss of contents by leakage. He was not in any sense a Pilgrim, as that term is applied by Bradford to his Leyden group who had wandered from England to Holland and then to our Plymouth. Bradford concludes his notice of Alden who "was free to go or stay" with this brief comment: "but he stayed." Doubtless his decision to remain can be connected with the famous courtship related in Longfellow's epic poem of which he expected to be the hero.

There was a surgeon unmentioned by Bradford whose

identity has been completely established. Bradford's failure to mention him is inexplicable as it is morally certain that he was in professional attendance on William Mullins in his last sickness. This medical man was Dr. Giles Heale, a member of the Company of Barber Surgeons of London where he served as an apprentice and became a freeman in 1619 and was licensed to practice there. He was, therefore, a young man just beginning his medical career when he was employed to accompany the *Mayflower* the next year. Whether he came out with an intent to remain as physician for the Plantation is unknown. At all events he probably returned with the *Mayflower* in April, 1621, and engaged in the practice of his profession in a house in Drury Lane, parish of St. Giles in the Field, London. There he continued his professional work until 1653 when he died. His will shows that he left a widow but no children. He witnessed the death-bed will of William Mullins in February, 1621, with Gov. Carver and the Captain of the *Mayflower*.

Another unidentified passenger of the *Mayflower* not mentioned by Bradford is a person called "Master" Leaver. He is named by Mourt's *Relation* (London, 1622) under date of 12 January, 1621, as leader of an expedition to rescue two Pilgrims who had been lost in the forest for several days while searching for thatch to roof their houses. In what capacity this person came in the *Mayflower* is uncertain and as his Christian name is not given, attempts at identification would be futile. The title of "Master," as well as heading the rescue party, indicates that he was a person of some authority and prominence in the company. He may have been one of the principal officers of the *Mayflower* and as nothing further is heard of him he probably returned, unless he died of the "general sickness" which then prevailed.

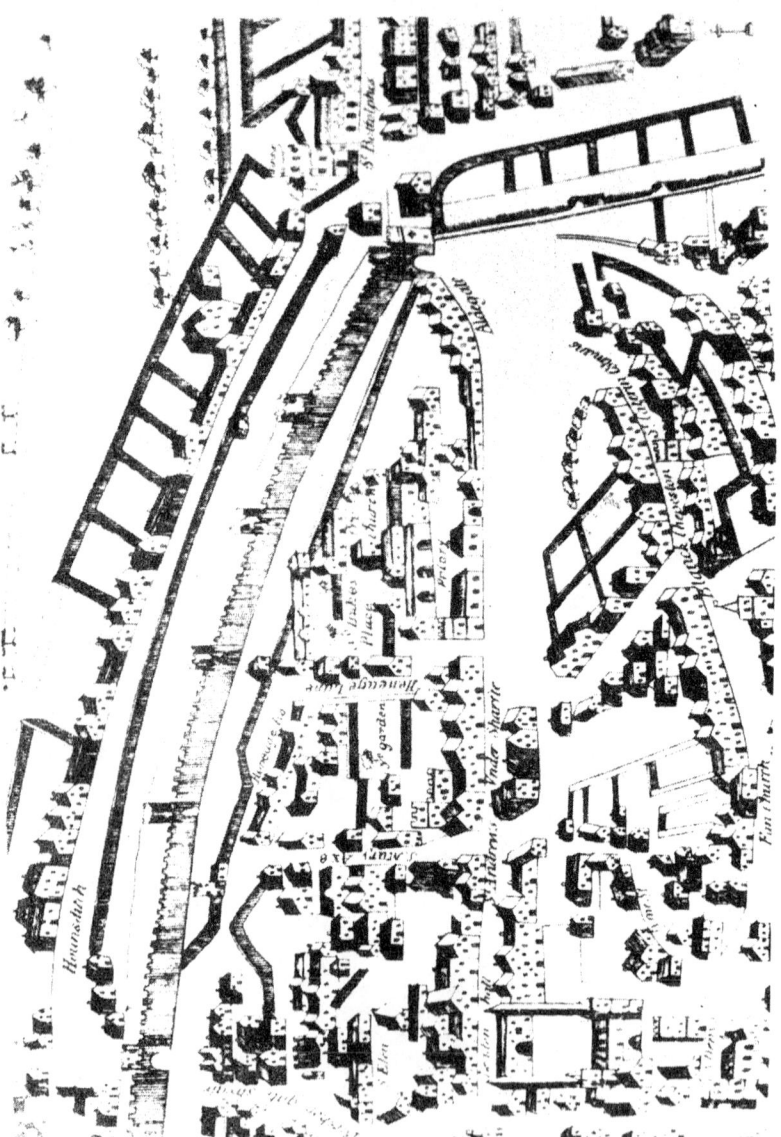

From a Contemporaneous Map of London, showing the Aldgate Triangle.

IV

LONDON AS A PILGRIM CENTRE

RESEARCHES by the compiler for material for this work make it clear that the seventeen persons credited to London in Dexter's list does not express the extent to which the great Metropolis was associated with the Separatist movement and the Pilgrim emigration. With the exception of Bradford and Brewster, the principal leaders of the Pilgrim Colony were of London origin and association. Winslow, Allerton, Hopkins, Warren, and probably Standish were among the great civil leaders of the Colony and they were the men who, as distinguished from the church element, gave stability to its financial management. None of the Leyden church members had ever shown any business capacity for large affairs. None of them had risen above the status of industrial workers. Bradford seemed to be the most successful of them and had acquired a house in Leyden which he sold for 1120 guilders, and when Carver died in the Spring of 1621 he was chosen to follow him as being, perhaps, the most successful member of the church financially.

As research developed it became clear that a definite area in London could be designated as a common source of Non-Conformist activity antedating the departure of the Robinson company to Leyden. The clue to this was found in Bradford's History in a letter which he incorported in his work, written by Robert Cushman who had been agent for the Pilgrims in their negotiations with the Merchant Adventurers of London, two years before the sailing of the *Mayflower*. This letter *(C.* VII, *page 43)* addressed:

> "To his lovinge friend Ed: Southworth at Henige House in the Dukes Place"

was dated 17 August, 1620, in Dartmouth harbor when Cushman was on the *Speedwell* bound for New England. The letter itself is of no historical significance but as it placed an early member of the Robinson-Brewster-Carver-Bradford group at a specified house in London it offered a clue which finally disclosed some highly important facts. This clue had been before the historical public for over seventy years but no one seems to have pursued it. The location of Heneage House, where Edward Southworth lived before and after 1620, was at the extreme East End of old London, in what was, and now is, known as the Aldgate Ward. Through this ward ran the old Roman highway consecutively known now from West to East as Holborn, Newgate, Cheapside, Poultry, Cornhill and Leadenhall streets, which continued by the Aldgate outside the City Walls as the Whitechapel Road and became the principal highway into Essex. The accompanying map will visualize the location to the reader. Heneage House was originally the town palace of the Abbot of Bury St. Edmonds in the Middle Ages and adjoined, and was part of, the great Priory of Holy Trinity which covered the apex of the Aldgate triangle, in the centre of which was a large court surrounded by monastic buildings.

When King Henry VIII dissolved the monasteries after his break with Rome, the Eastern half of this splendid property was bestowed on the powerful Duke of Norfolk and this portion of the ample gardens and picturesque courts of the Priory became known as the Duke's Place. The Western portion of the property, including the Abbot's palace, was bestowed upon Sir Thomas Heneage, whose name was attached to it, and the narrow lane which separated it from the other half of the property came to be called Heneage Lane which it still retains. The great house faced on Burys Marks (now corrupted to Bevis Marks), and just over the City Walls at that point was Houndsditch.

Edward Southworth had married in Leyden in 1613, Alice Carpenter and as this is his last record there it is probable that he removed soon after to London. By this marriage he became a brother-in-law of George Morton (who emigrated in the *Fortune*), and Samuel Fuller, the *Mayflower* passenger. Edward Southworth's selection of the Aldgate Ward for a home in London was not an accidental choice. Already it was the home of hundreds of Dutch craftsmen—members of the same religious organization which had welcomed him and the Scrooby exiles to Holland. A Dutch church had been established nearby and its records show many residents of the Duke's Place among its membership. In addition to this there were many French Huguenots, as early as 1600, who increased the alien population of Aldgate Ward until it rendered the properties of the Duke of Norfolk and the Heneage family unsuitable for residential purposes of the nobility. Both these owners turned their splendid buildings into tenements and in time they became like rabbit warrens for the teeming denizens of this locality. Thus we can understand how Edward Southworth, of the yeoman class, came to be living in this famous house.

A stone's throw from it is the church of St. Andrew Undershaft where an Allerton family lived at that period, with whom Isaac Allerton was undoubtedly connected. Also in this same parish the marriage of a John Tilley and the records of a Sampson family are found, all three of which are among the *Mayflower* passengers. The name of Britteridge (borne by one of the *Mayflower* passengers) is found in the parish of St. Katherine Cree to which Heneage House was parochially attached.

A short distance in another direction is the church of St. Katherine Coleman where a Stephen Hopkins family lived and it is known that the Pilgrim Stephen married his second wife at St. Mary Whitechapel just outside London Wall, beyond Aldgate. Here also in this ward was located the Guildhall of the Ironmongers Company, to which belonged Thomas Weston, the chief of the Merchant Adventurers who financed the voyage of the *Mayflower*. A quarter of a mile distant lived Thomas Prince, who came in the *Fortune* and was later Governor of the Plymouth Colony. Samuel Gorton, the famous religious pamphleteer who emigrated to Plymouth, lived in St. Botolph's parish, just outside Aldgate, while from the contiguous parishes of St. Leonard's, Shoreditch, and

St. Mary Whitechapel half a dozen of the Plymouth Pilgrims can be definitely traced. William Bradford is found there also in the Spring of 1620. He had sold his house in Leyden in April, 1619, and in the subsidy of March, 1620, his name appears as taxed for personal property at the Duke's Place which was a defined taxing district in that locality. Doubtless in anticipation of removal to the New World he had disposed of his property in Leyden and had taken his household goods and stock of fustian weaves to London preparatory to the great adventure. The significance of his residence there lies in the fact that he was with his old associates of the Scrooby company and that Mrs. Southworth became his second wife, three years later. Doubtless, his little son, John Bradford, who did not accompany the parents on the *Mayflower* was left in the care of the Southworths. It is the opinion of the editor of Bradford's History that Experience Mitchell, who came to Plymouth with Mrs. Southworth in 1623, also lived in that house or its neighborhood. The Mitchells were from the same part of England as Dorothy May, the first wife of Bradford, and possibly related.

The grouping of these associates in this locality was gradually developed by the compiler from many disconnected bits of circumstantial evidence which make up a complete and consistent picture. Numerous other corroborative facts, trivial in themselves, add illumination to the entire scene. The immediate region surrounding Heneage House and the Duke's Place maintained its atmosphere of Non-Conformity after the departure of our Pilgrims. In 1632 the Bishop of London, trying some of these Separatists and Brownists for contumacy, referred to Aldgate Ward as a "nest of Non-Conformists." Here was erected the famous Bury Street Chapel just back of Heneage House—the first Conventicle of these religious rebels who gave the Episcopal hierarchy so much trouble in that century.

Heneage House went the way of all medieval buildings a hundred years ago in the evolution of modern London. Not a vestige now remains of that "great House large of Rooms" where once these Pilgrim leaders—Bradford, Cushman, Mitchell and Southworth—lived and planned with Weston and Shirley (probably in Ironmongers Hall) the details and prospects of their epochal venture. The "fair Courts and Garden Plots" of Heneage House, described by Stowe, are now covered with business blocks and wholesale warehouses. The oldest Jewish Synagogue of the Restoration shelters a congregation professing that ancient faith on part of the original estate. The site of this interesting house is well known and its connection with such a tremendous event in the history of America and indirectly of the world marks it as a milestone of a pilgrimage which began in Scrooby and ended in our Plymouth. As such it may well be designated as the only Pilgrim shrine in London. It is more worthy of remembrance than the quays at Southampton and Plymouth, England, where brief stops were made, the last named port being an unintentional anchorage in the stress of navigating difficulties. The site of Heneage House calls for equal commemorative notice.

V

STORY OF THE *MAYFLOWER* AND HER MASTER

THE general facts concerning the voyage of the *Mayflower*, and like information regarding the ship itself, are matters of historic record; but some important and little known facts are here added to make the story of the Pilgrim ship complete. The certain history of the *Mayflower* dates from 1609 when she was employed as a wine ship trading at Mediterranean ports, being then owned by Christopher Nichols, Robert Child, Thomas Short and Christopher Jones. The last named was also her captain and the one who brought her with the first Pilgrims to New England. She was of about two hundred tons burthen and her home port in 1620 was London. Capt. Jones and Robert Child still owned their quarter shares in her, and it was from them that Thomas Weston chartered her in the summer of 1620 to undertake this epochal voyage.

She embarked about sixty-five of her passengers at London, probably off Blackwall or Wapping, about the middle of July and proceeded down the Thames into the English Channel and then on to Southampton Water, the rendezvous, where for seven days she awaited the coming of the *Speedwell*, bringing the Leyden church members, who had sailed from Delfts-Haven about the 22nd of that month *(Bradford)*. About August 5th, when all was in readiness, the two ships set sail for their destination. The unseaworthy *Speedwell* sprang a leak shortly after and they put into Dartmouth for repairs to "the leser ship." This having been accomplished, the second start was made. When "above 100 leagues without the Land's End" the captain of the *Speedwell* reported a continued leakage that threatened the safety of the ship and the two vessels were obliged to return and seek Plymouth harbor for rearrangement of the voyage and distribution of the passengers. The *Speedwell* was abandoned, a portion of her passengers transferred to the *Mayflower*, and others desiring to return to London did so. On September 16th, about a month after they first weighed anchor at Southampton, the *Mayflower* headed out to sea for the third time, and proceeded upon her historic voyage alone. After nearly eight weeks at sea she "arrived at Cap-Cod the 11 of November" *(Bradford)*, with one hundred and two persons on board—the same number who started—one having died and one birth balancing this loss. The officers and crew consisted of a captain, four mates, four quartermasters, surgeon, carpenter, cooper, cooks, boatswains, gunners and about thirty-six men before the mast, making a total of fifty, bringing the number of persons aboard the ship during the voyage to about one hundred and fifty.

The personnel, as far as known, enables us to make the following official roster:

CAPTAIN

Christopher Jones

MASTER'S MATES

John Clarke, *Pilot* Robert Coppin, *Pilot*
Andrew Williamson John Parker

GOVERNOR

Christopher Martin

SURGEON

Doctor Giles Heale

COOPER

John Alden

The names of the four quartermasters, cooks, gunners and boatswains are unknown.

Christopher Jones, her master, was a native of Harwich, co. Essex, England, born about 1570, the son of Christopher and Sybil Jones of the same parish, also a mariner and ship owner who died in 1578, leaving to the son bearing his name his interest in the ship *Marie Fortune* when he should attain the age of 18 years. Christopher, Jr., married (1) on Dec. 23, 1593, Sarah Twitt of Harwich, who died in 1603; and (2) in the same year Josian, widow of Richard Grey of Harwich. Capt. Christopher Jones was a man of considerable prominence in his community and was named as one of the burgesses of Harwich in the charter granted to that town by James I. In 1607 he was master of a ship called the *Josian*—probably named for his wife—but in 1609 he is first recorded as master of the *Mayflower* and one of the four owners of that vessel. From that period onwards he was continuously master of her up to the time when she was chartered by the Merchant Adventurers for her famous voyage. He removed to Rotherhithe, Surrey, about 1610, which became his home until his death. By his first wife he had one son. This child died in infancy. By his second wife, Josian, he had five children baptized in Rotherhithe 1611–1619 and a sixth child, John, baptized 4 March, 1620/1 at Harwich whither his wife had gone while he was on this voyage and in anchor in Plymouth harbor. After his return from New England in the Summer of 1621 he resumed his former trading voyages to Europe but not for long. It is evident that the perils and deprivations of the Pilgrim voyage had undermined his health as it did so many of the other voyagers, for on March 5th, 1621/2 he was buried in St. Mary's, Rotherhithe. Administration of his estate was granted to his widow August 26th following, but of the subsequent history of her and her young children nothing is certainly known. A Joan Jones, widow, married one Thomas Barthelmore in 1626 at Stepney, directly across the river from Rotherhithe. Christopher Jones left four sons—Roger, Christopher, Thomas and John—from whom it is possible that descendants still live who can trace their origin to the master of one of the famous ships of history.

When and where this ship of destiny was built is still an unsolved problem, but it is not improbable that she was launched at Harwich, and although later known as "of London" she was designated as "of Harwich" in 1609–11 in the Port Books. Two years after the death of Capt. Jones an application was made to the Admiralty for an appraisal of the ship by three of her owners at that time —Robert Child, John Moore and Mrs. Josian Jones. This appraisal was probably made to determine the valuation of the ship for the purpose of settling the estate of its late master, and four mariners and shipwrights of Rotherhithe determined her value as £128–08–04, about $5,000 at present relative values (*Pub. Rec. Off. H. C. A. 3, 81/167*). Her subsequent history has been the subject of much speculation and controversy. The author found in London hitherto unknown material which seems to have a direct bearing on the question. Robert Sheffield, a mariner of Stepney, London, living at Blackwall, by his will dated September 10, 1625, bequeathed to his wife Joan his part of "the good shipp called the 'Mayflower' of London being of the burthen of 200 tunnes or thereabouts" (*Commissary of London, xxiv, 646*). This language with its particularization accurately describes the Pilgrim ship. The small difference in tonnage from that stated by Bradford is negligible as both qualified the tonnage as "about" 180 and 200 tons, and it is well understood that such variations were common at that period. It is probable that Sheffield purchased the quarter share in the *Mayflower* of the widow of Capt. Jones.

Further discoveries by the author disclosed that the heirs of Sheffield in 1636 entered suit against one Simon Jefferson of Blackfriars, London, who had married Sheffield's widow in 1630, for an accounting of the property which was to revert to his children after the death of his widow. The heirs alleged that Jefferson refused to restore the reversionary interests according to the terms of the will, "including the part of the said shippe being worth one hundred pounds att the least." These hitherto unknown facts respecting this suit were found in the uncalendared records of the Court of Requests, Public Record Office, in bundles without arrangement of any sort, and the answer of the defendant (if any had been made) was not attached to the complaint (*Court of Requests, Charles I, Bdl. xi, part 2*). If this identification is accepted, the theory that the Pilgrim ship was captured in 1626 by the Dunkirkers will have to be revised. Sheffield died between September 10th and December 3rd, 1625, and at that date the plaintiffs in the Chancery suit aver that "at the time of his decease" Sheffield had an "adventure" in the *Mayflower*, and the inference from the pleadings in 1636 is that she was still in possession of Jefferson who refused to return the ship to the heirs. They did not ask for an accounting of the profits nor intimate that she was non-existant. From these documents it may be fairly claimed that the *Mayflower* was in existence sixteen years after her epochal voyage. The Port Books of England in the reign of James the First show that there were twenty-six vessels bearing the name of the Pilgrim ship, but the reason for the popularity of this name has never been explained. The identity of this particular vessel is based on her home port, her tonnage and the master's name in 1620. What finally became of her is an unsettled problem. Dr. Rendel Harris, an English historian of the Pilgrim ship, has published interesting material which he claims as proof that this historic vessel was finally broken up and her timbers used in the construction of a barn at Jordan's in Buckinghamshire.

PASSENGERS
OF THE
MAYFLOWER

CHRISTOPHER JOANES, *Master*

1620

THE MAYFLOWER

IN the following pages the names of the passengers are entered alphabetically and the new information which the compiler has obtained concerning them immediately follows, either in full, or in abstract, with supporting documentary references, to which has been added as occasion warranted certain other scattered facts obtained by others so that there will appear in compact form all new or known facts concerning the ancestry of each Pilgrim.

Of the 102 passengers of the *Mayflower* 25 are known to have left descendants and of these 15 were of the party of "strangers" from London and vicinity who left London in the *Mayflower* and joined the Leyden contingent who had come in the *Speedwell* to Southampton.

JOHN ALDEN

AS is well known, Bradford states that John Alden was a young man "hired for a cooper" at Southampton just prior to the sailing of the expedition. The municipal and parochial records of Southampton show several persons of that surname living in the city prior to 1600. The register of St. Michael shows the burial of a Richard Alden, 30 April, 1598, and the marriage of a "Wydoo" Avys Alden three months later. Evidently she was the widow of Richard. The Assembly Books of the corporation of Southampton show the name of George Alden, a fletcher (arrow maker) living in the parish of All Saints. His name appears regularly from 1587 to 1620 in the Court Leet Books of Southampton. Unfortunately, the early registers of All Saints do not now exist, but the Assembly Books show that he was surveyor of highways, 1600; a beadle in 1605; bondsman the same year (signing with a mark); surety for an alehouse keeper, 1619; with a last appearance of his name in July, 1620, in the stall and art lists when the *Mayflower* and *Speedwell* were lying at anchor in Southampton Water (*Assembly Books, pp. 16, 39a*). Jane Alden, a widow, was taxed in the city subsidy for 1628 *(P. R. O. 175/522)*.

From these records it is a fair presumption that John Alden, said to have been born in 1599, residing in

Southampton in 1620, may have been the son of George the fletcher, who disappeared—probably dying in that year—leaving John, an orphan, free to take employment overseas. Jane, the widow, may have been his mother and Richard and Avys his grandparents. His marriage with Priscilla Mullins, a fellow-passenger, derives some contemporary interest from the fact that a William Mullins and a George Alden were both in the tax list of Holyrood Ward in 1602 *(Assembly Book, fol. 1)*. It is left to the imaginative to infer that the famous romance of John and Priscilla began in Southampton.

The foregoing identification is incapable of proof, and is open to the objection that the name George does not appear in the families of John Alden or his descendants. The employment of John Alden "at Southampton" does not necessarily mean that he was a resident of that seaport as he may have only been at work there temporarily when the *Mayflower* arrived.

An equally probable and more plausible identification has recently been suggested to the author by B. Carlyon-Hughes, Esq., who is compiling a History of Harwich, England. It appears that an Alden family resided in Harwich, co. Essex, in the middle of the 17th century and that they were related by marriage to Capt. Christopher Jones of the *Mayflower*. They were engaged in seafaring pursuits and among them was a young John Alden of about the same age as the Pilgrim. This association through family connection can easily explain his employment "at Southampton." A Robert Alden was one of the Merchant Adventurers.

(See Gardiner.)

ISAAC ALLERTON

HE was called a tailor of London in the Leyden records, and was born in 1586, according to his deposition. There is nothing in his later career to show that he followed the occupation declared in the Leyden archives, although he may have been a tailor's apprentice. He became a merchant engaged in extensive trading in New England. As early as 1611 he was a resident of Leyden where he married Mary Norris of Newbury, co. Berks, for his first wife. In 1614, he was admitted as burgess of Leyden and it is worthy of note that Robert Allerton, called a "Scotchman," was living there contemporaneously with Isaac. None of the London registers nor the records of the Merchants Tailors Company of London give a positive clue to Isaac Allerton.

A Robert Allerton of St. Andrew Undershaft married a Grizell Playne in 1574 and had one son, John, baptized 1581, but no other entries of the name occur for twenty years. This seems the clue to his parentage. London wills afford no help. A Christopher Allerton was living in Bread Street, London, 1616, and an Edward Allerton of St. Dionis Backchurch was married to Rose Davis in 1579 but no issue is of record in that parish.

Bradford states that his son, Bartholomew, returned

to England and died there. A chancery suit of 1657 in which Bartholomew Allerton was a defendant relates to property in Suffolk, the parties being residents of Norfolk. It would seem that this son became a preacher, as the will of a Bartholomew Allerton, clerk, of "Bamfeild" (probably Bramfield) co. Suffolk, was proved in 1659. He mentions late wife Margaret, present wife Sarah and his "children" without naming them, unfortunately *(P. C. C. 92 Pell)*. The Hearth Tax of 1674 for Suffolk, containing 28,400 names—presumably every householder—does not contain the surname of Allerton, and on this negative evidence it may be inferred that his family had died out or removed to some other part of England. Allerton is the name of a parish in Northern Yorkshire and it is probably the origin of the family surname.

JOHN BILLINGTON

BRADFORD states that John Billington came from London, but none of the existing parish registers furnish confirmatory evidence. A Lawrence Billington of St. Botolph's, Aldgate, died in 1590 *(Arch. London, Act. Book 2/46a)*. There were Billingtons living in the parish of St. Mildred, Bread St., coopers, in 1640 *(P. R. O. Subsidy 251/22)*, and in the Tithe Report of London Householders in 1638 a "Widow" Billington is listed as a tenant in the parish of All Hallows, Stayning *(Lambeth MSS. Codex 272)*.

WILLIAM BRADFORD

THE ancestry of Governor Bradford has always been associated with Austerfield, Yorkshire, where he was baptized, but investigation shows that the earliest home of the family was Bentley-cum-Arksey, five miles from Austerfield (just north of Doncaster), in the same county, where they were settled as early as 1450, in the reign of Henry the Sixth and probably for many generations before. The Governor's line did not go to Austerfield until about forty years before his birth.

Robert Bradfourth of Bentley, born about 1450, appears to be the first of this line of record, taxed there in 1522, and dying the next year left three sons, of whom Peter is the next in succession, born about 1475, who was also taxed in 1522, and died twenty years later. His will dated 17 January, 1542, and proved 19 March, 1542, mentions seven sons and there were two daughters besides, of whom Robert, born about 1500, is the direct ancestor of the Governor. He owned lands in Bentley, Arksey; Tickhill, Stansell, Wilsyke and Wadworth, adjoining parishes, which he bequeathed by will, dated 28 November, 1552, proved 5 October, 1553, to his nine children, by two wives. He lived at Wellingly, parish of Tickhill, and as this hitherto unidentified name reappears at Plymouth, it was undoubtedly bestowed by the Governor in memory of a family residence, familiar to him in his boyhood. His father dying when he was scarcely a year old, and his mother remarrying when he was only three, it is probable that he was brought up with near relatives in Wellingly. William Bradford, the eldest son of Robert, was the first of the Bradfords to remove to Austerfield, about 1557, probably becoming a tenant of the manor, but it was not until 1576 that he bought a freehold estate there of Anthony Morton, Esquire *(Feet of Fines, Yorks, 19 Eliz. Trinity)*. He was twice married, and by first wife (name unknown), had four children, among whom was William, born about 1560, father of the Governor. The elder William died in 1595, surviving his son William four years.

William Bradford, the father of the Governor, married 21 July, 1584, Alice Hanson, daughter of John and Margaret (Gresham) Hanson of Austerfield, of a family which appeared in Austerfield the middle of the 17th century. She was baptized 8 December, 1562, and the issue of the marriage was Margaret, b. and d. 1585; Alice bapt. 1587, and William bapt. 19 March, 1589/90, the Pilgrim Governor. His father died and was buried 15 July, 1591, and his mother married Robert Briggs, 23 February, 1593, and thus by the death of his grandfather and father, and remarriage of his mother in the space of four years he was left almost bereft of his natural guardians. It is certain that he inherited from his grandfather a house and about ten acres of land in Bentley and the presumption that he may have gone there to live with relatives, or was brought up by them seems to be supported by his bringing the name of Wellingly to Plymouth rather than Austerfield. As far as known no resident of the latter parish can be associated with the Leyden company, while Bentley, Tickhill, Arksey and Doncaster show evidence of such connection, being adjoining parishes.

The compiler found in the Public Record Office, London, the original Fine, dated 1611, by which Bradford sold his inheritance in Bentley, consisting of a house, cottage, garden, orchard and nine and a half acres of land, and to complete this legal transaction he must have gone back to England from Leyden. He makes no mention of this in his History, nor of his removal to London, the year before the sailing of the *Mayflower*, as related in Chapter IV, *ante* pp. 11–16.

In the parish of Bentley-cum-Arksey there lived another Bradford family who were armigerous, but there is no known connection between the two. The other family originated in Wakefield, co. Yorks, and their armorial bearings are shown in the contemporary publications. It is possible that the two families had a common ancestor many generations back of the Governor's line. It is well known that his first wife, Dorothy May, belonged to an armigerous family of that name in Cambridgeshire, but as far as known the Bradfords of Bentley and Austerfield were only well-to-do yeoman stock.

WILLIAM BREWSTER

EXHAUSTIVE search has added some light on the early origin of the family of this important leader of the Pilgrims. Brewster is a vocational surname found mostly in the North of England as applied to one who brews ale and beer. In the South of England it appears as Brewer in the same way that Webber is found in the Southern and Webster in the Northern counties. From the earliest time when tax lists were available Brewsters are found in the Scrooby region and in the neighboring parishes of Yorkshire where the earliest generations of Bradfords resided. The Subsidy of 2 Richard II (1379) shows a Robert Brewster taxed in Bawtry which adjoins Scrooby. The will of a William Brewster of Bentley-cum-Arksey was probated in 1521 and another William Brewster was taxed in the same parish in 1524. This latter William could be the grandfather of "Elder" William and father of the William who was appointed steward and bailiff of the Manor of Scrooby. There seems to be no good reason why the Archbishop of York should have gone to Essex, as suggested by some writers, for this official when Brewsters were then living within his own diocese in the neighborhood. These early Brewsters of Bawtry and Bentley seem the logical and most hopeful clue to the ancestry of the spiritual guide of the Plymouth Pilgrims. It has long been known that a Rev. Henry Brewster was Vicar of Sutton-cum-Lownd, when the "Elder" was born, and that a James Brewster in 1584 was appointed Master of the hospital of St. Mary Magdalene, Bawtry; and that both of these parishes are close to Scrooby. James became Vicar of Sutton in 1596 and Scrooby was in his parochial cure. This curious combination of persons bearing the same name may be more than accidental, but it has never been satisfactorily explained.

Elder Brewster's father, as steward of the Archbishop's Manor, gave him a certain social status which was reflected by the son when he matriculated at Cambridge University, and following this his employment in the diplomatic service by Sir William Davidson undoubtedly caused the officials of the High Court of Commission, who summoned him for religious contumacy in 1607, to address him as "William Bruster of Scrowbie, gent." At present there is nothing to show that he was a "generosus" (*i.e.*, well-born) in the social estimation of the period.

The date of his marriage is important although it is not known whether the wife Mary who accompanied him to Leyden and Plymouth is the mother of his children. Her identity has so far eluded search. If she were the second wife the following records of marriages of men of his name may be possible clues: William Brewster and Mary Welles June 21, 1599 (St. Mary Woolchurch, London); William Bruster and Mary Scrobs Jan. 24, 1604 (Stoke Bruern, Northants), and William Brewster and Mary Morden December 22, 1608 (St. Peter Eastgate, Lincoln). It has been suggested that Mary, daughter of Thomas Wentworth, Esq., of Scrooby Manor may have become his wife *(Burgess, Life of John Robinson, p. 81)*. The will of Thomas Wentworth, 27 March, 1574, mentions a daughter Mary, evidently the eldest, but without indication whether married or single.

As Brewster was born about 1563-4 he would have married ordinarily about 1585, but being abroad then in the diplomatic service this event was delayed until after his return to England, in all probability. He severed connection with Davidson in 1587 and was discharging the duty of Post at Scrooby in the early months of 1589 as an assistant to his father, then incapacitated and who died intestate the next year *(S. P. Dom. Eliz.* ccxxxiii: *48)*. The son was appointed administrator of his estate, 24 July, 1590, the widow Prudence refusing to act. As the office of Post was in reality that of a tavern-keeper, where the King's Post-riders changed horses and travelers were accommodated with meals and lodging, it is certain that William Brewster required a wife to assist him in the domestic needs of such an establishment. His mother was probably too old to continue these responsibilities. It is probable that he was married without much delay if indeed he was not already married, being then 25 or 26 years of age. Bradford, in his imperfect account of Brewster, which lacks many essential facts, said he had "many children." We only know of five, of whom Jonathan, b. 1593, is the oldest, and five children are not "many." With a wife near his own age there would be time for the births of ten children in her productive life and this would answer the required "many" of Bradford's account *(fol. 255)*. That he had a son older than Jonathan is certain. Between the probable date of his marriage (1587) and the latter's birth (1593) there was room for three children. The ages of the four other children—Love, Wrestling, Fear and Patience—are figured as born between 1595 and 1605.

The records of the Virginia Company of which Sir Edward Sandys was President, and whose son Samuel leased the Manor of Scrooby to Brewster, show that William Brewster and his son Edward bought shares (1609) in that enterprise. This would be a natural thing for William Brewster to do, and ten years later the Leyden Church Company intended to go to Virginia under the protection of Sandys. In the summer of 1619, Brewster was in London, secretly, hunted both in Holland and England by order of King James for publishing a seditious book. Sir Robert Naunton, Secretary of State, had charge of the search for this fugitive, and on 1 August, 1619, he wrote to the British Minister at The Hague that "Brewster is frightened back into the Low Countries." Two days later he wrote: "Brewster's sonne, of his ffather's sect within this halfe yeare, now comes to Churche" and he adds that he had "recovered a note from him (Brewster) to his sonne, and comitted the deliverer close untill hee discover where the ffather is" *(S. P. Dom. James I, 110)*. This son of the Elder was not the Edward who went to Virginia, as he was on trial there in August, 1619, and sent back to London for political reasons, while the Elder's son at that date was reported as abandoning his father's sect and being reconciled to the Established Church. A confusing fact in this connection is the existence of an Edward Brewster, an apprentice of the Stationers Company in London, learning the trade of a printer which the Elder was following in Leyden. He became a freeman in 1615 and his first publication registered in 1616 was entitled "A Lowe Countrye trayning." This combination of surname, occupation and place identical with the Elder's life at that time seems startling, if it be accidental. Edward, the London printer, published between 1616 and 1640 twenty-five books, all of them sermons or on religious controversy. An Edward Brewster was Master of the Stationers Company in 1692, probably a son of the earlier Edward.

Nothing has been learned regarding the family name of Prudence, the mother of Elder Brewster. There is no clue on which to base a search unless it may be found in the guardianship which Elder Brewster held over Anne Peck, a young woman of Lownd near Scrooby who had accompanied him in the flight to Holland. She was a sister of Robert Peck, and as relatives were usually chosen as guardians it may mean that she was related to his wife or his mother *(Leyden Records, Groot Proc. Bk. D.* XVI *230).* Anne Peck married John Spooner in 1616, and Peter Powell in 1631, both at Leyden.

RICHARD BRITTERIDGE

HE was probably from London but as he died shortly after the landing on December 21st evidences of his English origin are only of indirect importance. A Brightridge family lived in South Shoebury, co. Essex, in 1624; another in Prittlewell nearby, and the name of Britteridge is found in the parish of St. Katherine Cree, London, contemporaneously; which was the parish church of the Duke's Place in which Heneage House was situated and thus in close contact with Southworth, Bradford and Mitchell.

PETER BROWNE

THIS Pilgrim was a brother of John Browne, the weaver of Plymouth. He died about September, 1633, leaving only three female descendants. His origin has not been identified but as there was a Peter Browne taxed at Great Burstead, co. Essex, in 1624, which is the parish in which Billerica is located, whence came a number of *Mayflower* passengers, it is not unlikely that this may be the clue to his English home.

WILLIAM BUTTON

HE was a youth, servant of Samuel Fuller. He died at sea when near the coast of New England and offers no special interest to the genealogist.

Davis states that he was son of Robert Button and baptized at Austerfield 12 February, 1598 (*Original Narratives of Early American History, p. 94*).

ROBERT CARTER

HE was servant to William Mullins and in the will of the latter is spoken of as one "who hath not so approved himself as I would he should have don." He died in the first winter without issue and probably came from London or vicinity.

JOHN CARVER

GOVERNOR CARVER, one of the early associates of Brewster and Bradford, and brother-in-law of Rev. John Robinson, should be looked for and found in the region whence these leaders of the Scrooby group originated. This supposition proved to be more than probable as he is undoubtedly identical with the John, son of Robert Carver, baptized 9 September, 1565, at Doncaster, Yorkshire. It should be borne in mind that this parish is only seven miles distant from Austerfield and it is next to Bentley, the earlier home of the Brewsters and Bradfords.

He married Mrs. Catherine (White) Leggatt, widow of George, and daughter of Alexander White of Sturton-le-Steeple, Nottinghamshire. Her sister Bridget became the wife of the pastor of the Pilgrim church at Leyden. They had no issue but brought with them on the *Mayflower*, Desire Minter, three men servants, a maid servant and a boy transported under his care. Carver died about April or May, 1621, aged fifty-six years, and his wife followed him shortly after.

His only known signature, found by the compiler in the probate files of the Archdeacons' Court for Surrey, is that shown on the will of William Mullins as a witness as well as the writer of the body of that document.

JAMES CHILTON

HE is believed to be identical with James Chylton, citizen and tailor of Canterbury in 1583. The following entries from the church register of St. Paul, Canterbury, record the baptisms of his children, viz.: Isabella, 15 January, 1586; in 1615, she married Roger Chandler in Leyden, later of Duxbury (1632); Jane, 8 June, 1589; "Ingle" 1599. He removed to the parish of St. Martin, same city, and had the following children baptized: Elizabeth, 14 July, 1594, and James, 22 August, 1596. Two other children—Mary and Joel—died in 1593 there.

The following entries from St. Peter's, Sandwich, undoubtedly refer to the same James (the parish where several of the Pilgrims lived prior to removal to Leyden) viz: Christian, 26 July, 1600; James, 11 September, 1602; Mary (famous for her historic leap making her the first to land on Plymouth Rock) was probably born about 1608 in another parish. Convincing proof of this historic performance may be read in "Mary Chilton's Title to Celebrity" by Charles Thornton Libby (privately printed, Boston, 1926, octavo pp. 27). James Chilton died shortly after the "Landing."

The name Chilton occurs in the Leyden records but the items relate to Isaac Chilton, a looking-glass maker, said to be from France. He may have been a son of James. Angela Chilton married Robert Nelson in 1622 at Leyden, probably the "Ingle" above named.

RICHARD CLARKE

HE died in the first general sickness in the winter of 1621 without issue and the surname is too common for any serious suggestions of identification.

FRANCIS COOKE

SUCH information as relates to this Pilgrim will be of a negative character and the space devoted to disposing effectually of the fantastic story of his birth and relationships found in a recent publication. "New Light on the Pilgrim Story," Chapter 6, entitled "The St. Francis of the *Mayflower*," (p. 55) contains the baptism of a "Francisca" Cooke, alleged to be identical with the *Mayflower* Pilgrim, and makes the statement that he was so baptized at St. Martin's in the Field, London, 27 October, 1578. In order to support this claim the authors argue that the name "Francisca" was written in ignorance by the parish clerk of that period "who had no knowledge of either Latin or Italian" and used the feminine terminal letter "a" when it should be the masculine letter "o"! I pass over the incorrect Latin opinion of the authors to say that this curious argument is built upon a false premise. The original record at St. Martin's reads: "Mris Francisca Cooke," baptized on the day stated, showing that the authors deliberately omitted the prefix "Mris" (*i.e.*, Mistress) which proves that this person of quality was a female, and that it was not the clerk of the parish who was ignorant of Latin, or of the sex of the person baptized. If there is any explanation of this vital error which disposes of the entire Chapter 6, "The St. Francis of the *Mayflower*," it should be made in the interest of historical accuracy. It might also be added that in the same register "Francisca Cooke," presumably the same person, was buried in 1591. It can, with equal propriety, be assumed that even if identity were established a person of the same name having been buried in 1591 could not be the emigrant of 1620.

If nothing definite has been found about this Pilgrim, it is at least profitable to clear his record of such an unwarranted investiture of nobility, of which he was in supreme ignorance. Possible clues to his identity may exist in the following: a Francis, son of Thomas Cooke, was baptized 6 April, 1572, at Biddenden, Kent. Another Francis Cooke in a chancery suit recites his misfortunes in business through dishonest servants and losses in trade (*Court of Requests, James I, Bdl.* vi, *Pt. 3*). The Leyden records give his betrothal 9 June, 1603, and this presumes his birth 1582 or before. After reading the entry in the Betrothal Book where he is recorded as "Franchois Couck" and his bride Hester Mahieu, and noting that the witnesses to his marriage were two Walloons and his wife probably of that race, it is fair to express a doubt as to his own nationality. He may have been born in England of alien parents and returned to Holland six years before the arrival of the Robinson Pilgrims. There was a considerable alien French and Walloon colony in Canterbury which occupied the crypt of the Cathedral for church services.

As he was living in Leyden seven or eight years before the arrival of Robinson and his followers it is clear he had no prior association with the Pilgrims.

HUMILITY COOPER

ACCORDING to Bradford, Humility Cooper was a "cousin" (*i.e.*, niece), of Edward Tilley and his wife, which can be interpreted as a niece of Mrs. Ann Tilley, for John and Edward were brothers and the reference to relationship is solely to Edward. As she was unmarried and returned to England, where she died, no genealogical interest could be served by an endeavor to locate her origin. She was probably from London.

She had one acre granted to her in 1623 adjoining that of Henry Sampson, both of them being relatives of Mrs. Ann Tilley.

JOHN CRACKSTON

HE was one of the early victims of the "general sickness" of the first winter and died leaving issue. He was one of the Leyden contingent and is credited as from Colchester, co. Essex. A John Craxon is found in the subsidy of 1624 at Hawkwell, Essex, a few miles from Prittlewell where a Britteridge family is found. It is known that Crackston left descendants. According to Davis, "his wife was probably a Smith" (*Landmarks, Pt. 2, p. 74*).

His son John survived and his "heirs" were mentioned in later years in the divisions of land.

EDWARD DOTY

EDWARD DOTY (Doughty) was from London and came as a servant of Stephen Hopkins, also from that city. The register of St. Mary-le-Strand, London, gives the marriage of an Edward Dowty and Wynifryd Waryner, 12 December, 1613, and the marriage of a Thomas Dowghty four years later. As Bradford refers only to Doty's second marriage this London record may possibly be his first wife though the interval is rather lengthy. Thomas is a name found in the Plymouth line. An Edward Dowtie was a juror of Southwark in 1629 *(Ancient Indictments, Kings Bench)*.

Thomas Doughty, born in 1575, was a draper in the parish of St. Martin's, Orgar *(Exchequer Depositions, Mich. 17, 44/5 Eliz.)*. A Richard Dowty, clerk of St. Saviours, Southwark, made his will in 1555 *(Arch. Surrey)*. These suggestive clues should furnish groundwork for successful investigation.

FRANCIS EATON

FRANCIS EATON was a carpenter by occupation and the compiler suggests that he was ship's carpenter of the *Mayflower* employed by the Merchant Adventurers. The following entry from the Corporation Records of Bristol indicates that Eaton was from that city:

"John Morgan son of Edward Morgan of the City of Bristol, sailor, deceased, apprenticed to Francis Eaton of the City of Bristol *carpenter* and Dorothy his wife for seven (7) years, paying 4s 6d for the liberties of Bristol with two (2) suits of apparel and one suit 'telorum pertenr ad artem le carpinter.'"
Marginal Note: "The Mr at New England."
(*On the back of the indenture.*)
"The Master consenteth at the end of the said term to convey to the apprentice and his heirs forever 25 acres of land lying in *New England* in America and also to give unto him 15 bushels of wheat he serving him truly the term of his apprenticeship. (*Bristol Apprentice Book, Vol. 1626–1640 fo. 23.*)"

As there was no other known Francis Eaton, carpenter, at that period in New England this must be considered a definite clue.

THOMAS ENGLISH

THOMAS ENGLISH was hired to go as master of the *Speedwell* and is therefore assumed to have been a resident of Leyden. He died in the first winter without issue. He appears in the Leyden records as Thomas England.

MOSES FLETCHER

H E was a smith by occupation and is credited to Leyden as his residence at the time of the emigration. He died in the first winter without issue as far as known. The parish register of St. Peter's, Sandwich, co. Kent, gives the baptism of Moses, son of Moses Fletcher, 10 October, 1602, and as this was the church where Richard Masterson with his brothers and sisters lived 1594/1610, later of Leyden and still later of Plymouth, this record undoubtedly refers to Moses Fletcher, the Pilgrim.

EDWARD FULLER

E DWARD FULLER with his wife and children have been satisfactorily identified in the genealogies of this family. Edward was baptized 4 September, 1575, as son of Robert, a butcher of Redenhall, Norfolk. There is no record of him at Leyden and it is probable that he joined his brother Samuel at Southampton.

SAMUEL FULLER

THIS Pilgrim was called a serge maker of London (*Gemeente Archief, Leiden*), but it is of record that he added the practice of medicine and surgery to his later activities in the Plymouth Colony. Thomas Morton, the incorrigible author of "New England's Canaan," makes sport of this occupation, calling him the son of a butcher. Morton credits his English residence as Wrington, co. Somerset, but this evidently was an error for the home parish of his second wife, Agnes Carpenter, whom he married in Leyden, 15 March, 1613. His third wife was Bridget Lee, daughter of Joyce Lee and sister of Samuel Lee,—whom he married 12 May, 1617, at Leyden. William Hoyt was his brother-in-law. Samuel Fuller was baptized 20 January, 1580, Redenhall, co. Norfolk.

RICHARD GARDINER

RICHARD GARDINER was a seaman employed by the Company to remain, but returned to England and left no further traces. He was probably son of John and Lucy (Russell) Gardiner of Harwich, co. Essex, and related by marriage to Capt. Christopher Jones. It was a sea-faring family.

(See Alden.)

JOHN GOODMAN

JOHN GOODMAN came from Leyden and died without issue the first winter. The statement which appears in the Dunham Genealogy that this was a name assumed by Deacon John Dunham, a later emigrant, as a mask to hide his identity, is an absurd suggestion without the slightest documentary evidence. In fact, it is completely disproved by the Leyden records.

WILLIAM HOLBECK

WILLIAM HOLBECK came as a servant to William White and died without known issue in the first winter. The name of Holbeck is found in St. Andrew's parish, Norwich, where the Rev. John Robinson had a curacy before his removal to Leyden. He is to be credited as one of the Leyden contingent.

JOHN HOOKE

JOHN HOOKE, servant to Isaac Allerton, died in 1621 without known issue in the "general sickness." He is credited as one of the London contingent, the name not being found in the Leyden records. A John Hooke is found in the parish of St. Giles, Cripplegate, in 1600 and another of the same name lived in the parish of St. Bartholomew the Great early in the year in which the *Mayflower* sailed.

(See Bumpus, Martin, Rogers.)

STEPHEN HOPKINS

THE known and already published facts concerning this Pilgrim that are factors in his identification are his previous residence in London (*Mourt's Relation*) and the name of his wife, Elizabeth, stated to have been his second marriage (*Bradford*). The church register of St. Mary Matfellon (Whitechapel) records the marriage of Stephen Hopkins and Elizabeth Fisher, 19 February, 1617/18, which complies with the necessary factors just quoted. This places Hopkins in the parish on the highroad entering London at Aldgate near which Bradford, Carver, Cushman and Southworth lived in or near Heneage House, Aldgate Ward, as already shown, and thus provides the atmosphere and propinquity required to establish this probability. The name of his first wife is not known but he may be the same Stephen Hopkins, a resident in the parish of St. Stephens, Coleman St., who had a son Stephen, baptized 22 December, 1609, possibly by this first marriage. All other Stephen Hopkinses found in London have been followed to a point where they could be eliminated from consideration as the Pilgrim.

It seems possible to identify the Pilgrim, Stephen Hopkins, with one of his name who sailed for Virginia in the *Sea Adventure* which set sail 15 May, 1609, via Bermuda and was wrecked on the shore of that island. This earlier Hopkins, in an account of this voyage, is described as one "who had much knowledge in the Scriptures and could reason well therein." The chaplain of the party chose him to be his assistant "to read the Psalmes and Chapters upon Sondayes" after they had become settled on the island. The narrator continues the story of this stranded company (which was originally bound for Virginia) and relates a mutiny among the passengers who were desirous to continue the voyage. This Stephen Hopkins was one of the ringleaders. Sir George Summers caused these mutineers to be arrested and tried. Hopkins with his associates was found guilty of rebellion, "but so penitent hee was and made soe much moane alledging the ruine of his Wife and Children," that upon the plea of the rest of the company the Governor pardoned him. After this a small bark was built and the company proceeded to Virginia. (*Purchas. His Pilgrimes, Book ix, pt. 2; comp. Gen. Reg. xxxiii, 305.*)

The significance of this and its connection with Stephen Hopkins, the Pilgrim, will be apparent from what is recorded of him after arrival of the *Mayflower* at Plymouth. He was of the first exploring party sent out to seek a suitable place for habitation and while on this errand they came across a sight which was curious to them —a small tree bent over and attached to boughs and grasses woven together covering a deep pit. Hopkins at once informed them that it was a trap used by the Indians to catch deer. Knowledge of this sort was not the common property of residents of London but must have been acquired by previous residence among the Indians such as we know was the case with the Stephen Hopkins on the 1609 voyage. Doubtless he had seen the same device in Virginia. When Samoset came to Plymouth and welcomed the Pilgrims he was lodged overnight in Stephen Hopkins' house, doubtless because Hopkins could understand his language and converse with him. When the messenger of Canonicus brought the snake-skin full of arrows to Plymouth, Standish and Hopkins had charge of him (Standish in his capacity as military commander), and tried to get at the meaning of the message this snake symbolized. As Standish did not know the Indian language, Hopkins was chosen to learn from the Indian what it meant. In 1623 Hopkins accompanied Winslow on the mission to Massasoit just as he did in 1621, doubtless for the same purpose—his knowledge of the Indian tongue. These instances definitely confirm the view that Hopkins had been on this coast prior to his voyage on the *Mayflower*. It was always Hopkins when negotiations with the Indians were necessary and he could not have learned these things in London. It seems highly probable that Weston selected Hopkins to accompany the Pilgrims because of his previous knowledge of this coast.

One clue remains to be considered—the rare name of Giles, his son. The compiler has only found one instance of it—that of a Giles Hopkins, a tiler of Bristol, living there in 1639, aged 44 years. It is to be remembered that Francis Eaton also came from Bristol. The Militia list for Gloucestershire, 1608, shows a family of weavers and clothiers in the hamlet of Wortley in the parish of Wotton under Edge (16 miles from Bristol) bearing the names of Stephen Hopkins and his sons. Unfortunately, the parish records of Wotton are imperfect for the years necessary for identifying our Stephen as of this family, but sufficient exists to show the baptism of a son William to Stephen Hopkins, 19 July, 1607, after which the name disappears from the register. Theoretically, this gives opportunity for the removal of this Stephen to London in time to join the *Sea Adventure* on her voyage to Bermuda as above related. An imperfect entry in the Wotton register records the baptism of —— Hopkins of Stephen Hopkins, 29 October, 1581, who was the fourth child and whose age would fit that of the Pilgrim. The record does not state whether a son or daughter, but as no child had been named Stephen for himself possibly this was the name of the child.

(See Sampson.)

JOHN HOWLAND

JOHN HOWLAND, who was born about 1594, came as a servant of John Carver, but as there is no record of his residence in Leyden he is credited to London for the reason that Carver was in England for some considerable time before the sailing of the *Mayflower* and undoubtedly obtained the services of Howland in that city prior to the departure from England. The Howland ancestry is probably of Essex origin. The will of Humphrey Howland, citizen and draper of St. Swithin's, London, in 1646, mentions his brothers, John and Arthur, which are known Christian names of this family in New England, at the date of the will. There was a John Howland taxed at Canfield Parva, Essex, 1623, and the name also occurs earlier at Newport Pagnall in the same county. In London a John Howland was living in the parish of St. Mary, Whitechapel, in 1596, and in 1600 another John belonged to the parish of St. Botolph, Billingsgate. Jeffrey Howland was taxed in 1625 in the parish of St. Botolph, Aldgate. These parishes are all close to or part of the Pilgrim quarter of London.

JOHN LANGMORE

JOHN LANGMORE as servant of Christopher Martin was of the London contingent but possibly originally a resident of Essex at the time of his embarkation with his master. He died the first winter in the "general sickness" without known issue.

WILLIAM LATHAM

WILLIAM LATHAM, a "boy," came as servant to John Carver. He was taxed in Plymouth in 1632 and later resided in Duxbury. He returned to England after 1641 and later emigrated to the Bahamas *(Bradford)*. He left no known issue.

EDWARD LESTER

EDWARD LESTER, or Litster, came from London as the servant of Stephen Hopkins, completed his apprenticeship in Plymouth and then removed to Virginia (*Bradford*). It is not known that he left any descendants in the latter colony but as no investigation of this is of record it is possible that *Mayflower* descendants of this passenger may be found in the Old Dominion.

An Edward Lister, widower, of Ixworth, Suffolk, married a second wife in 1590 and may be the father of the Pilgrim passenger. This name is very uncommon.

An Edward Lyster of St. Mary Aldermanbury was married 2 May, 1614, to Ann Walthall, widow, of St. Peter, Cornhill.

There was a Lister family living in the parish of St. Mary, Kensington (a suburb of London), 1586–1607, having the name of Edward among the children, and this place may be the clue to the origin of this Pilgrim.

EDMUND MARGESSON

EDMUND MARGESSON died without known issue in the first winter of the "general sickness." A John Marginson lived in the parish of Bentley-cum-Arksey, Yorkshire, where Gov. Bradford lived. An Edmund Margetson is found in 1603 in the records of Gimmingham, Norfolk. There is a possibility that this name may be an error for Edmund Masterson who was father of Richard Masterson of Leyden who came to Plymouth later.

CHRISTOPHER MARTIN

THIS Pilgrim was the "Governor" of the *Mayflower*, and according to Bradford "came from Billirike in Essexe, from which partes came sundrie others to goe with them." With him came his wife, Marie Prower, a widow whom he had married 26 February, 1606/7, at Great Burstead, Essex. She may have been the widow of John Prower, a laborer of Hockley, co. Essex (a parish a few miles distant from Billerica) or perhaps his daughter-in-law. Martin and his wife died without known issue the first winter in the "general sickness." On 3 March, 1619/20, Martin was prosecuted in the Archidiaconal Court "for suffering his son (Solomon Prower) to answer him (*i.e.*, the Archdeacon) that his father gave him his name." *(Gen. Reg. 21. 77).*

(See Prower.)

DESIRE MINTER

THIS young woman came as a member of the family of John Carver and after his death returned to England and died there unmarried, as far as known. She may be related to a William Minter of Norwich who emigrated to Leyden and was granted citizenship there in 1613. He died before 1618 leaving a widow, Sarah, who was daughter of Thomas and Alice Willett of Norwich. The latter were the parents of Thomas Willett who came to Plymouth in 1629 and, as is well known, became the first Mayor of New York City.

There were families of that name in Essex and Suffolk living contemporaneously with this passenger.

RICHARD MORE

HE deposed in 1684 "aged seaventy yeares or thereabouts" that he was living in the house of Mr. Thomas Weston, ironmonger, in London in 1620, "and was thence transported to New Plymouth in New England" *(Gen. Reg. L, p. 208)*. This is, of course, the Thomas Weston who was the chief instigator of the emigration and the leader of the Merchant Adventurers who financed the voyage of the *Mayflower*. In the parish of Shipton, co. Salop, the register shows the baptisms of the children of Samuel More, "generosus," by his wife Catherine as follows: Elinor, 24 May, 1612; Jasper, 8 August, 1613; Richard, 13 November, 1614. As the latter date agrees with the age of Richard More and the names of Elinor, Jasper and Richard are those of the three children (transported) and the family name of More disappears from the Shipton Register this identification seems reasonable. A family named Tilley lived in the same parish (*q.v.*). His sister Elinor and brother Jasper died the first winter in the "general sickness." Before accepting absolutely the identification above suggested it is to be noted that a Jasper More resided in Gilston, co. Herts, and was married there in 1569 and another Jasper More lived in Devonshire in 1615, being instances of the existence of persons bearing the same name in different parts of England contemporaneously.

WILLIAM MULLINS

AS father of the famous Priscilla, this Pilgrim has a certain romantic background which deserves such particularization as facts concerning him have been developed. The annotation in the probate record of his will *"nuper de Dorking defunctus in partibus transmarinis"* implies that he formerly lived in Dorking, co. Surrey. Conclusive record of his residence in that parish cannot be established. The Dorking Register shows baptisms, marriages and burials of persons named Mullyns 1571/1585, after which there is a hiatus of a quarter of a century before another entry occurs. William Mullins had a holding in the Manor of Dorking which he bought in 1612 and for which he paid an unusually large rental of 23 shillings per annum. He had paid £122 for this and in May, 1619, sold it for £280 to one Ephraim Bothall. A significant entry is found in the records of the Privy Council, 29 April, 1616, when a warrant was issued to bring "one William Mollins before their Lordships." On May 1st he appeared before the Privy Council and was continued technically in their custody "untill by their Honours' order hee be dismissed." The cause of his arrest is not stated but it can well be assumed that it was on account of the religious controversies of that period, and the sale of his property three years later seems to be a logical sequel. There is no evidence, however, that he was one of the Leyden religionists and he is confidently placed among the London contingent. His will shows that he held nine shares in the Adventurers Company and that his estate consisted principally of a stock of boots and shoes. It is apparent that William Mullins was beyond middle life when he emigrated as he left behind him a married son and a married daughter in Dorking, undoubtedly by a first marriage. His daughter, Priscilla, and youngest son, Joseph, were issue of the second wife, Alice, who accompanied him on the *Mayflower*. William, Jr., the eldest son, was married by 1617, as three of his children were baptized in Dorking, and he himself was a later emigrant in 1636 to New England. The elder daughter Sarah was also married before her father emigrated and as Sarah Blunden she administered his estate, with will annexed. The name Blunden does not occur in the Dorking register although it is found occasionally in the records of the county of Surrey.

Assuming that William Mullins the Pilgrim was 50 years of age when he emigrated he may be identical with the William Mullins residing in 1596 at Stoke, near Guildford, co. Surrey (Muster Roll) about ten miles from Dorking.

His will, the first made in New England, written by Governor Carver and witnessed by him and Dr. Giles Heale, surgeon of the *Mayflower*, and Captain Christopher Jones, is reproduced as a frontispiece to this volume.

DIGORY PRIEST

DIGORY PRIEST is credited as one of the Leyden contingent although he was originally called a hatter from London in the Leyden records. He married Sarah (Allerton) Vincent, widow of John Vincent of London, 4 November, 1611, and was admitted a burgess four years later *(Gemeente Archief, Leiden)*. The name of Digory Priest or Prust is common in Devon and Cornwall. A family with these names in Lezant, co. Cornwall, offers promising field for investigations as to the earlier origin of this emigrant. He died the first winter of the "general sickness," aged about 42 years, leaving two daughters, Mary and Sarah. Families of this name were living in the parishes of All Hallows the Great, All Hallows on the Wall, St. Augustine, St. Dunstan-in-the-West and St. Margaret Patten in London at the period of the emigration.

SOLOMON PROWER

SOLOMON PROWER came from Billerica in the family of Christopher Martin as the stepson of the latter. He died in the first winter of the "general sickness" without known issue. On 3 March, 1619/20, he was haled before the Archidiaconal Court at Chelmsford, Essex, for refusing to answer Archdeacon Pease: "Who gave him his name in baptism? And he answered he did not know because his father was dead and he did not know his God-father's name." *(Chelmsford Archidiaconal Records.)* He was discharged.

(See Martin.)

JOHN RIGDALE

JOHN RIGDALE with wife Alice was undoubtedly from London. The name Rigdale and Ragdale are found in a number of London parishes of that period. Both died in the first winter of the "general sickness" leaving no known issue.

THOMAS ROGERS

THOMAS ROGERS and Joseph, his son, are credited to the Leyden contingent but it is suggestive that the names of Christopher Martin, Thomas Rogers and John Hooke are found early in 1620 as taxpayers of the parish of St. Bartholomew the Great, London. Thomas, the father, died the first winter in the "general sickness," but his son survived and descendants now bear the name. (*Bradford.*) He was called a "camlet merchant" in the Leyden records and appears to have come to Leyden a few years before the migration as it was not until 1618 that he acquired citizenship. He was guaranteed by William Jepson who was from Worksop, Notts, and Roger Wilson of Sandwich, Kent. If either was a neighbor or relative, clue to his origin may be found here. Bradford says (*page 453*) that Thomas Rogers had other children beside Joseph who came in the *Mayflower*. He states that they came over later but their names are not on the Leyden records. He sold his house there in April, 1620, preparatory to removal to America.

HENRY SAMPSON

HENRY SAMPSON was of the London contingent and was designated as "cousin," *i.e.*, nephew of Edward Tilley and his wife. This probably means a nephew of Mrs. Edw. Tilley as he is not so specified in relationship to John Tilley. As two of his children bore the names of Stephen and Caleb which appeared contemporaneously in the Hopkins family it is probable he was related either by marriage or blood to Stephen Hopkins. A Sampson family was resident of the parish of St. Andrew Undershaft, London, where a John Tilley was married in 1605 *(q.v.)*.

GEORGE SOULE

THIS Pilgrim, the maternal ancestor of the compiler, is credited to the London contingent in which he came as a servant of Edward Winslow. He has been tentatively identified as son of John Soule of Eckington, co. Worcester, and probably kinsman to Robert Soule, a wealthy London salter, who died in 1590 a native of Eckington. Robert Soule had a son Miles and a grandson of George, the emigrant, also bore that name. All other George Soules found in England at that period have been satisfactorily eliminated. Fuller particulars of this identification will be found in the recently published Soule Genealogy for which a special extensive search covering a number of years was made by the compiler of this book.

The Winslow family from which Edward was descended lived in the nearby parish of Kempsey, co. Worcester, and it is probable that this early neighborhood association explains the apprenticeship of George Soule to the Governor. It is supposed that George Soule was in London when he joined Winslow on the voyage. Droitwich, the family home of the Winslows at that time, was a salt mining place connected in a business way with the Salters' Company of London in trade, and thus the Winslow-Soule association was established.

The name of Mary Bucket, his wife, who came in the *Anne*, should be looked for in the parish of St. Botolph, Aldersgate, London. It is probably a variation of Beckett. The marriage is established through the sale by George Soule of that acre of land granted to her as a passenger, which he could do as her husband.

MYLES STANDISH

THIS name, perhaps the best known and the most famous of all his fellow-passengers, has successfully defied and still defies all efforts to establish his English residence or parentage. The statements in his will reciting his supposed heirship by remainder in certain specified lands in Lancashire practically identifies him as of the Ormskirk branch of the Standish family in that county. His statements that he was the rightful heir of a "second or younger son *from* the house of Standish of Standish" has been misinterpreted as it does not mean technically *of* the house of Standish of Standish. There were several distinct branches of that well-known family in that county and the Standishes of Standish Hall had no estate in the six parishes named by him in his will, viz.:—Ormskirke, Burscough, Wrightington, Maudesley, Croston and Isle of Man.

Although an almost nation-wide search has been made for the record of his baptism and every existing parish register in Lancashire has failed to produce the information in the county where he is said to have been born (*Morton, New England's Memorial*), this does not necessarily mean that such a record is non-existent as the author has been given credible information that an English vicar a generation ago told his informant that he had found the record; it was in his possession and that he intended to make it public in a special article. As this plan never materialized the information either died with him or possibly remains among the posthumous papers of this vicar, in possession of his descendants.

It is the belief of the author that Capt. Standish was of London origin or residence in youth, and in consequence of the possible death of his mother, or that his father died early, leaving him an orphan, and thus without a trade he became a soldier of fortune. Capt. John Smith said that he was "a bred Souldier in Holland" (*Generall Historie, p. 247*) and Hubbard amplifies that statement thus: "Captain Standish had been bred a soldier in the Low Countries and never entered the school of our Savior Christ or of John (the) Baptist, His harbinger." (*History of New England, III.*) A contemporary writer, who knew Standish personally, has left on record a statement that he was "a quondam drummer," probably meaning that Standish began his military service in Holland as a drummer (*Morton, New England's Canaan, 141*).

The author spent the best part of a year in England searching every available Standish clue in all classes of records but without adding anything to our present knowledge.

ELIAS STORY

ELIAS STORY came as a fellow servant with George Soule in the family of Edward Winslow from London. It is a question whether this name is not Stery or Sterry. Bradford, writing in 1650, thirty years after the landing, could hardly be expected to remember accurately the correct spelling of the names of the young men-servants who died unmarried in the first winter as did Story. The name Story in Bradford's original manuscript shows a blotted o or e, and the unusual name of Elias found in the Sterry family of London seems to point to it as the correct name of this passenger.

The will of Thomas Sterry, citizen and goldsmith of London in 1578, made a bequest to his son Elias Sterry, and as that baptismal name is of great rarity and the surnames alike in appearance the question is raised as to Bradford's possible error. As the Pilgrim Story or Sterry died in 1621 leaving no issue the answer is of no genealogical importance except as every individual identification assists in locating associates.

EDWARD THOMPSON

EDWARD THOMPSON was a servant of William White and died shortly after arrival at Cape Cod. As he left no issue any effort to locate him would be useless. Nothing is known of his antecedents.

EDWARD TILLEY

EDWARD TILLEY was from London and undoubtedly had been associated with Thomas Weston, the Merchant Adventurer, prior to joining the *Mayflower* party in London. Edward Tilley has been identified as the son of Lawrence and Bridget Tilley, baptized 29 October, 1574, at Shipton, co. Salop. This is the county from whence Weston undoubtedly came and the name Tilley disappears after 1616 from the parish register. Edward and his wife Ann both died in the first winter of the "general sickness."

The compiler regards this identification of Edward Tilley as disproved for reasons which will be explained under the name of the next passenger, John Tilley, his brother.

(See Sampson, Cooper.)

JOHN TILLEY

JOHN TILLEY has been identified as an older brother of the preceding Edward as baptized, 24 February, 1571, and perhaps the son of Lawrence and Bridget Tilley of Shipton, co. Salop, and the same remarks apply to him as to the correctness of this conclusion. Both John and his wife died in the first winter in the "general sickness" leaving but one known child, Elizabeth, who married John Howland. The compiler found a marriage of a John Tilley to Elizabeth Comyngs, 2 February, 1605, in the parish of St. Andrew Undershaft, where an Allerton family resided, and close to the Pilgrim center there. As Elizabeth, daughter of the Pilgrim, was born in 1607 this record may be the marriage of the *Mayflower* passengers.

The compiler is obliged to reject the identification of these two brothers announced a quarter of a century ago (*N. Y. Gen. & Biog. Rec. XXXV, 213 291*) by a writer who adopted the Shipton record as evidence satisfactory to himself. A Chancery deposition, found by the compiler, in the Public Record Office, N. 7/14, was made by John Tylly of Shipton, Salop, yeoman, in 1631, aged 60 years, hence born in 1571 and therefore identical with the John baptized as above stated. It shows that the Shipton John supposed to have emigrated on the *Mayflower* and dead in 1621, was still alive ten years later living in his native parish. This automatically eliminates his brother Edward. A John Tilley, yeoman, was living in Wootton, Bedfordshire, in 1613, aged 40 years, hence born 1573, and this may be the emigrant. (*Chanc. Deps.* T. *5/16*.)

(See Allerton, Britteridge, More.)

THOMAS TINKER

THOMAS TINKER with wife and son are credited to the Leyden contingent and as all three died in the first winter there are no known descendants. There were Tinkers in Tickhill, co. York, where the Bradfords lived and it is probable that they were of the part of the original Pilgrim band who emigrated to Leyden under the leadership of Bradford and Brewster. A Thomas Tinker, carpenter, of Neatishead, co. Norfolk, born in 1581 at Thurne, same county, may be the Pilgrim.

WILLIAM TREVOR

THIS sailor was employed to remain with the Company for one year and was undoubtedly engaged for his knowledge of the coast. He had been one of the crew of Capt. Dermer's ship in his voyage of the previous year. He came over in later years as master of a ship and made a deposition concerning his previous voyages to the coast. (*Bradford I, 270, II, 150, 401.*)

JOHN TURNER

JOHN TURNER with wife and two sons came to Plymouth and are classed with the Leyden contingent. All died in the first winter, but a daughter came some years after to Salem and married there. *(Bradford.)* Her identity has not been established. In 1592 a John Turner sold a messuage in Doncaster to William Bradforth and it is probable that the *Mayflower* Pilgrim was of the original Pilgrim band in 1610 emigrating to Leyden with Bradford and Brewster. John Turner, a merchant, was admitted burgess of Leyden that year.

A John Turner was married at Whitechapel in 1615, where later Stephen Hopkins took a second wife. Several persons connected with the Pilgrims lived in that parish.

RICHARD WARREN

RICHARD WARREN came from London and was called a "merchant" of that city *(Mourt)*. Extensive research in every available source of information—registers, chancery and probate in the London courts, proved fruitless in an attempt to identify him. As he died before 1628 it is probable that he was considerably past middle life at the date of emigration.

A careful analysis of the reading of Bradford's statement about Richard Warren in the section devoted to "Decreasings and Increasings" justifies the compiler's belief that Mrs. Elizabeth Warren, who came over in the *Anne* in 1623, was his second wife. After stating that "his wife came over to him" he adds the significant statement *"by whom* he had two sons before (he) dyed." After stating the "increase" he adds: "but he had five daughters more come over with his wife" which can only be accurately read as his children and not hers. His separation of the sons, who were the specific issue of the wife Elizabeth, from the daughters who came over with the wife completes the picture of family relationships. As she survived him for nearly half a century, dying in 1673, it is almost conclusive confirmation of this theory. An estimation of the probable dates of birth of the five daughters, based on the known facts, gives the following result: Mary, born 1606; Elizabeth, 1608; Anne, 1612; Sarah, 1614, and Abigail, 1616.

Richard Warren, a London haberdasher, was licensed to marry Elizabeth Evans of St. Mildred Poultry, 1 January, 1592/3, at St. Leonard's Shoreditch, and a Richard Warren married Marjorie Jordan, 1 September, 1606, at St. Martin's in the Field. Either one of these might be the *Mayflower* Pilgrim.

St. Leonard Shoreditch parish adjoins that of St. Botolph without Aldgate and St. Mary whitechapel, from both of which came Pilgrims, and Nicholas Snow has been identified as of St. Leonards *(q.v.)*. It is in the heart of the Pilgrim area in London. The records of the Honorable Artillery Company of London, 1612, contain the admission of a Richard Warren as a member that year but no further information is available as to his identity.

WILLIAM WHITE

IN connection with this Pilgrim further reference must be made to "New Light on the Pilgrim Story," Chapter 15, entitled "A London Puzzle," in which the distinguished Rev. John White, D.D., Rector of Barham, Suffolk, is made to pose as the father of William White of the *Mayflower*. The authors also make this statement unreservedly: "In his will he mentions his son who had left his church and his country." This is an error. The original will of Dr. John White neither mentions a son William nor anything about any son leaving "his church and his country." The only reference in the will to theological matters is his description of his own struggles against the Romish doctrine and his controversial pamphlets on this subject.

As one of the Leyden company in 1612 he is described as a wool carder in the record of his betrothal to Susanna Fuller. His surname being one of the dozen commonest names in England and his baptismal name one of the four most frequently bestowed in that period, grounds for identification are lacking. The name Peregrine given to his son born during the voyage of the *Mayflower* may be of the same character as Oceanus given to the Hopkins child, as Peregrine indicated one born during the time his parents were traveling. Peregrine is an exceedingly rare Christian name and is perhaps best found in the family of Lord Willoughby (Bertie) who lived in that period. In the Protestation Roll of Dorset, 1641, the name of Peregrine White occurs in the parish of Beaminster and if this be a coincidence it is certainly a curious one.

ROGER WILDER

ROGER WILDER came as a servant to John Carver and died in the first winter without known issue.

THOMAS WILLIAMS

THOMAS WILLIAMS, who died in the first winter without known issue, offers slight hope of identification as the name is so common. He and his sister lived in Leyden and they were called of Yarmouth, co. Norfolk.

EDWARD WINSLOW

NOTWITHSTANDING the subsequent prominence of this Pilgrim, definite and undisputed facts regarding his ancestry are strangely wanting. It is known that he was baptized 18 October, 1595, as son of Edward Winslow of Droitwich, co. Worcester, by his wife Magdalen Oliver whom he married the previous year at St. Bridget's, London. Edward, the father, according to a family record, was born 17 October, 1560, and was undoubtedly a descendant of the Winslow family of Kempsey, Worcestershire, which existed in that county before 1500. The Winslow estate in Kempsey was called Kerswell and the name was given to the Winslow estate in Plymouth as Careswell. It is highly probable that this Edward, Sr., was the son of a Kenelm Winslow of Kempsey, or of a contemporary Richard Winslow of the same parish. Kenelm Winslow, probably a brother of Edward, Sr., born in 1551, was called a resident of Worcester, yeoman, in 1605 and is probably the one whose will of 1607 bequeaths property to his eldest son, other children and grandchildren, without naming them.

The will of Thomas Harton of Kinsham, parish of Bredon, 1620, in scheduling his bad debtors names among them Edward Winslow, a deputy sheriff of Worcestershire, who had fled to Ireland *(Soame, 114)*. This may refer to the father of the Pilgrim. In 1614 when Winslow was only 19 years of age he was called a printer of London in the record of his betrothal in Leyden to Elizabeth Barker of Chattisham, Suffolk *(Gemeente Archief)*. In 1624 when in London he made a deposition, aged 30 years, calling himself "yeoman" and deposed that he took £60 of stock in the Plymouth adventure.

The coat of arms usually shown in engraved portraits of Gov. Winslow and elsewhere have never been properly authenticated.

PASSENGERS

OF THE

FORTUNE

Thomas Barton, *Master*

1621

THE FORTUNE

THOMAS WESTON, who financed the voyage of the *Mayflower*, wrote as follows to Governor Carver about the setting out of this second ship, the *Fortune*, not knowing at that time of the death of the Governor. Weston informed him that "Mr. Beachamp and myself bought this little ship and have set her out, partly, if it may be to uphold the plantation as well to doe others good as our selves; . . . This is the occasion we have sent this ship and these passengers, on our owne accounte."

Governor Bradford gives the following account of the arrival of this ship and some information about the passengers:

"In November, about ye time twelfe month that themselves came, ther came in a small ship to them unexpected or looked for (she came ye 9 to ye Cap) in which came Mr Cushman (so much spoken of before) and with him 35 persons to remaine & live in ye plantation; which did not a little rejoyce them. And they when they came ashore and found all well, and saw plenty of vitails in every house were no less glade. For most of them were lusty yonge men, and many of them wild enough, who little considered whither or aboute what they wente, till they came unto ye harbore at Cape-Codd, and ther saw nothing but a naked and barren place. . . . So they were all landed; but there was not as much as biscuit-cake or any other victialls for them neither had they any bedding, but some sorry things they had in their cabins, nor pot, nor pan, to dress any meate in; nor over many cloathes, for many of them had brusht away their coats & cloaks at Plimoth as they came. But ther was sent over some burching lane suits in ye ship, out of which they were supplied. The plantation was glad of this addition of strength but could have wished that many of them had been of beter condition, and all of them beter furnished with provissions."

There can be little doubt that the passengers of the *Fortune*, with the few exceptions noted in their proper places, were gathered together in London by Weston and his partner. Although Bradford states that there were thirty-five persons, the names of but twenty-eight are known as receiving lots credited to those arriving in the *Fortune*. Eighteen are known to have been unmarried, eight married, but emigrating without their families; and, as far as known, Mrs. Martha Ford was the only woman on the ship, but it is probable that the missing seven in the count of passengers were wives. Bradford, however, does not leave that impression in his account.

The individual records which follow make it clear that sixteen of the passengers can be definitely assigned to London, Stepney or Southwark, and only three from Leyden. Ten more, whose origins cannot be stated, died early or left the Colony.

JOHN ADAMS

HE was called a carpenter, probably from London. A John Adams, son of John, sailor, was baptized 30 April, 1590, at St. Botolph, Aldgate, and another John, son of John, a baker, was baptized 7 August, 1595, in the same parish. A John Adams was taxed at Norton Folgate (Shoreditch), 1596, on goods in the subsidy of that year. These parishes were right in the heart of the Puritan district whence came others on this ship. John Adams of Ratcliffe, mariner, married Susan Lane, 7 October, 1619, at St. Dunstan's, Stepney. It should be noted that John Adams of Plymouth had a daughter Susan. He died in 1633 and his widow Ellen married (2nd) Kenelm Winslow. As he had but one acre allotted him in 1623 he was either single at that date or his family did not come with him.

WILLIAM BASSETT

HE was a gunsmith and worker in metals, and is probably the William, son of William Bassett of Bethnal Green, London, next Whitechapel, who was baptized at Stepney, 24 October, 1600. Extended investigation satisfactorily disposes of the inference that he was identical with a William Bassett of Leyden twice married before 1612 and said to be from Sandwich, co. Kent. The church records of Sandwich, all parishes, do not confirm this supposition. The emigrant's death in 1667 and the terms of his will indicate that he was not old enough to have been a widower in 1611, as was the Leyden William, who was a "hodman" (mason?). Bethnal Green was in the Pilgrim neighborhood whence came Hopkins, Warren and Snow. He was unmarried on arrival, but in the division of 1623 was allotted two acres showing that he had taken a wife before that date.

WILLIAM BEALE

THERE is no further record of this passenger in Plymouth as he did not share in the 1627 division and either died or left the Colony. His allotment of one acre in 1623 indicates that he was unmarried at that date.

JONATHAN BREWSTER

HE was a ribbon maker, son of "Elder" William, born at Scrooby in 1593; for his English origin see under Brewster, p. 35. He was twice married, first about 1610 (name unknown) who died May, 1619, in Leyden; second, Lucretia Oldham, in 1624, called of Derby, a sister of John (see under *Anne*), or related to Margaret Oldham of Leyden (1611).

CLEMENT BRIGGS

HE was a fellmonger, and in 1616 resided in Southwark, co. Surrey, with Robert Hicks, a fellow-passenger, as appears in a deposition dated 29 August, 1638. He was unmarried on arrival and having only one acre granted in 1623 shows that he was still single at that date. His name does not appear in the subsidy of Southwark for 1620 but parish registers of St. Saviour or St. George will probably disclose information of his family there. Perhaps the adjoining parish of Bermondsey may furnish facts.

(See Hicks.)

EDWARD BOMPASSE

THIS is a name of French derivation but he probably came from London as a John Bumpas was living in the parish of St. Bartholomew the Great in 1620 *(Subsidy 147/505)*. Another John Bumpasse, gardener, lived in Battersea across the Thames on the South Side of London (*P. R. O. Court of Requests* LXIV—*Pt. 1, temp. Charles I*). He was unmarried on arrival and also single in 1623 at the division of land that year. He was probably one of the "lusty yonge men" in this ship.

Robert Bumpus was a householder in 1638 in the parish of St. Andrew Holborn, London, near St. Bartholomew.

(See Hooke, Rogers, Martin.)

JOHN CANNON

THERE is no family record of this passenger in Plymouth as he did not share in the 1627 division and either died or left the Colony. He was unmarried on arrival and still single in 1623 at the division of land that year. The name is not found at Leyden and he undoubtedly came from London.

As this name is given as both Carman and Cannon in the records, it may be added that a John Carman was living in Stepney in 1640, and it is quite probable that this is the returned passenger of this ship.

(See Tench.)

WILLIAM CONNER

HE was unmarried on arrival and in 1623 was still a bachelor as shown by the land division that year. He did not share in the 1627 division of cattle and had either died or left the Colony before that date. The name is not found in the Leyden records.

ROBERT CUSHMAN

HE was a wool carder, living in Canterbury and Rolvenden, co. Kent, son of Thomas and Elinor (Hubbard) Couchman of Rolvenden, where he was baptized 9 February, 1577/8. He became a prominent official in the Leyden Church; married (1) Sarah Rider, 31 July, 1606, at St. Alphege, Canterbury; (2) Mrs. Mary Chingleton (or Singleton), widow of Thomas of Sandwich, 3 June, 1617, at Leyden. In 1624 Robert Cushman deposed aged 45 years, calling himself a yeoman residing in Rosemary Lane, London *(High Court of Admiralty Records, Bk. 44)*. Rosemary Lane, Whitechapel, now Royal Mint Street, was in the Pilgrim neighborhood before noted. He was Agent of the Pilgrims in London, 1617–1626, doing excellent service to the great advantage of the Colony. His visit to Plymouth in the *Fortune* was for observation only, to ascertain the needs of the Plantation, and while here he preached a sermon that was printed after his return. His descendants in the United States are through his son Thomas (born 1607), who came with him in the *Fortune*.

STEPHEN DEANE

BY occupation a miller. Was unmarried at arrival and probably one of the "lusty yonge men." He died young (1634) leaving three daughters, having married in 1627 Elizabeth Ring, from Leyden. Nothing has been found to identify his English origin, but there are some reasons for thinking he came from Southwark.

PHILLIPE DE LA NOYE

AS the name indicates he was of French origin, and only 16 years of age when he arrived (deposed in 1641 aged 36 years). He must have been at this time a servant of one of the other passengers, being a minor. In 1634 he married Hester Dewsbury and died in 1681/2.

Edward Winslow stated that de la Noye "came to us from Leyden, born of French parents, who coming to age demanded also communion with us" *(Good Newes &c)*.

THOMAS FLAVEL

HE was one of the older married passengers as his wife came in the *Anne* two years later. He did not share in the 1627 division and had either died or left the Colony before that date. A son was with him in 1623 at the division of lots. He was probably from one of the suburbs of London. A Flavel family lived in the Tower Division in 1620, and Thomas Flavel married Elizabeth Hayward, 22 July, 1610, at St. Saviour's, Southwark. The name being very uncommon, it is more than probable that this is the record of his marriage, as most of the passengers of this ship came from London. (See Pitt.)

(———) FORD

THIS nameless passenger is assumed to be the husband of Martha Ford, of whom Mourt records this event: "the Goodwife Ford was delivered of a son the first night she landed, and both of them are very well" (*Relation*, *p. 13*). This disposes of the supposition that she was a widow, as commonly stated. It must be assumed, however, that the husband died shortly after arrival, as the widow married Peter Brown, the *Mayflower* passenger. She received four lots in the 1623 division, to which she was entitled by this family count. Her two Ford children shared in the 1627 division of cattle, after her second marriage. Extensive search has failed to locate the prior marriage of a Ford to a maiden bearing the prenomen of Martha . . . , but this surname is very common in most of the counties of England.

A William, son of William Ford, leather dresser, was baptized in 1615, and as Southwark furnished a number of emigrants both in the *Fortune* and the *Anne*, it is not improbable that this may be a clue to the origin of this passenger.

WILLIAM HILTON

HE was the son of William and Ellen Hilton of Northwich, co. Chester, where he was living with his wife and children, 1616–20, but at the time of emigration he was undoubtedly resident in London with his brother Edward. Both are called Fishmongers *(Hubbard)* but this is not verified by the records of that company in the case of William. Edward who had been apprenticed to Marie, the widow of Charles Hilton of the Fishmongers Company in 1611, became a Freeman of that Guild before emigration. The letter of William Hilton describing the natural resources of the new country, dated shortly after his arrival, was printed in Smith's "New England's Trials." His wife and two children, William, baptized 22 June, 1617, and Mary, baptized 11 May, 1619, came in the *Anne*, 1623, and were allotted three shares in the division of 1627.

Religious controversy arose in Plymouth on account of the baptizing of a child of William Hilton by the Rev. John Lyford, and Hilton removed to New Hampshire in 1623/4 where, with his brother Edward, he founded the present city of Dover.

ROBERT HIX (HICKS)

HE was a fellmonger, of London, residing at Southwark in 1616. He had been married before emigration, but he drew only one lot for himself in the 1623 division. In 1627 his wife Margaret and four children participated in the division of 1627. His name does not appear in the Subsidy of 1620 for Southwark, but the parish registers of St. Saviour and St. George should give some record of his family. The adjoining parish of Bermondsey furnishes the following information relating to baptisms of his children, viz.: Thomas, 19 February, 1603/4, (bur. April, 1604); John, 12 October, 1605; Sarah, 25 October, 1607. As there are no further entries in the register he probably removed to Southwark after the last-named date. Robert Hix was born about 1570.

(See Bangs, Briggs.)

BENEDICT MORGAN

HE was a sailor, a resident of St. James, Clerkenwell, London, when he emigrated, and was born in 1597 (*P. R. O. High Court of Admiralty Records, Bk. 44*). He married Agnes Porter, 22 November, 1619, and had one lot assigned in the 1623 division. He returned to England in the *Anne* and did not again come to New England. He was buried 8 October, 1630, "a poore man" *(Parish Records)*, leaving several small children. The assignment of one lot in 1623, although a married man, is proof that land was only given to those who actually emigrated—one acre to each person.

THOMAS MORTON

HE is stated by Morton Dexter to be a brother of George Morton who came in the *Anne (q.v.)*, perhaps the Thomas Morton baptized 1 March, 1589, at Austerfield, co. York, the home of Bradford. (See under passengers of *Anne*, Thomas Morton, Jr.) As he had but one share of land in 1623, he came alone.

A(UG)USTIN(E) NICOLAS

THERE is no family record of this passenger in Plymouth as he did not share in the 1627 division and either died or left the Colony. The name indicates that he may have been of Flemish origin. His share of one acre in 1623 indicates that he came without a family.

WILLIAM PALMER

THIS Pilgrim was a nailer by occupation and one of the older passengers, as he died in 1637, having grandchildren. He mentions Stephen Tracy of Leyden in his will and a grandchild Rebecca who may be identical with Stephen Tracy's daughter of that name. This may be an indication that he was related to someone who belonged to the Leyden Church. He arrived without any of his family and they had not come to Plymouth in 1623, when he was granted one lot. In 1627 his wife Frances and son William shared in the division of cattle. He was probably born about 1570 and his wife must have been much younger.

The evidence that he came from London is quite strong. He had a servant called "Carvanyell" and this odd surname is found in Stepney. There are records of marriages between the Palmers and Bassetts at St. Mary, Whitechapel, the adjoining parish.

WILLIAM PITT

THERE is no further record of this passenger in Plymouth as he did not share in the 1627 division and either died or left the Colony. He had come as a single man or without a family as in 1623 he drew but one lot.

It is probable that the marriage of William Pitt of St. Peter ad Vincula, Tower of London, armorer, in 1625 (after he returned) to Susan Flavel of Stepney is that of this emigrant and connects him with a fellow-passenger, Thomas Flavel (*q.v.*).

THOMAS PRENCE

HE was the son of Thomas Prince of All Hallows, Barking, London, carriage maker, and had just reached his majority when he emigrated. His father had lived at Lechlade, Gloucestershire, before coming to London, but the parish records, such as survive in transcripts, do not indicate that this was the original home of the family. Interesting contemporary letters concerning the father and grandfather of Governor Prence are in the collections of the Massachusetts Historical Society. Thomas Prince, Senior, of All Hallows, in his will of 1630 mentions "my son Thomas Prence now remayninge in New England in parts beyond seas" (*P. C. C. 70, Scrope*). As he bequeaths a "seale Ringe of Gold" to his son, it may be presumed that the family was armigerous. The future Governor was brought up in the neighborhood whence came so many of the passengers of the first two ships, and the *Mayflower* must have taken her passengers in sight of his home, near the Tower.

The proper spelling of this surname is Prince and it was so written by his immediate and collateral forebears, but he chose to write it as Prence. He lived in the hamlet of Ratcliffe, parish of Stepney, as a boy and probably remained there with his parents until his emigration.

MOSES SIMONSON

HE was a member of the Church at Leyden, of Dutch descent, of whose origin no information has been obtained beyond this fact. He came as a single man, being granted an acre in 1623, and possibly was a minor when he emigrated as it was not until 1633 that he became a freeman. Edward Winslow stated that "Simonson was a child of one that was in communion with the Dutch Church at Leyden" *(Good Newes from New England)*.

HUGH STACIE

HE was a yeoman, probably unmarried at arrival. Nothing has been learned of his origin, but there was a Hugh Stacie of Blewberry, co. Berks, 1644, which may be a clue to the home of the family *(P. C. C. "Rivers")*. He drew one lot in 1623 and is probably identical with one of the same name who was of Salem, 1639; Dedham, 1640, and Salisbury, 1642. As he was not a freeman until 1642 he may have been brought over as an apprentice by one of the other passengers.

JAMES STEWARD

THERE is no further record of him at Plymouth after 1623, as he did not share in the 1627 division, and he either died or removed from the Colony. He was either unmarried or without a family on arrival as he had but one lot assigned him.

WILLIAM TENCH

NOTHING is known of this passenger prior to emigration. Beyond the assignment of land in 1623, and the sale of land before 1630 jointly with John Cannon or Carman, the records are silent. Probably died without issue. The name suggests London origin, as it is of frequent occurrence in that city. Having but one lot assigned him in 1623 he was unmarried at that date and no subsequent records indicate that he had a family.

The Plymouth Colony Records (*XI. 54*) state under date of 1638 that William Tench and John Cannon "did bequeath two acres of land" to John Billington, deceased, which his widow and son sold. This may indicate some relationship between these people.

(See Cannon.)

JOHN WINSLOW

H E was brother of Edward, of the *Mayflower*, and baptized 18 April, 1597, as recorded at Droitwich, co. Worcester (see under Winslow, in the list of *Mayflower* passengers for his ancestry). He was unmarried on his arrival and in 1623 had but one acre assigned him. He married Mary Chilton *(q.v.)*.

WILLIAM WRIGHT

THIS is such a common name that identification cannot be suggested with confidence. He evidently married Priscilla Carpenter, as he calls Governor Bradford "brother" and Samuel Fuller calls him "brother," and both of them had married daughters of Alexander Carpenter. It would indicate that he was connected with the Leyden congregation before emigration. He was one of the older passengers, married, and died in 1633 (*Register* IX, *35*). He may have been one of those left behind in 1620, but in view of the London origin of so many in this ship, the printed parish registers of that city, and the wills in the local courts at Somerset House (*Archdeacon, Commissary and Consistory Courts*) should be examined.

Having but one acre in the division of 1623 he came alone in this ship.

A William Wright, son of William, was baptized at Austerfield 10 March, 1588, and this may well be the Pilgrim.

PASSENGERS
OF THE
ANNE
WILLIAM PEIRCE, *Master*
1623

THE ANNE

BRADFORD gives the following particulars of the company of emigrants who came in this ship: "About 14. days after, (*i.e.*, July 10, 1623), came in this ship caled the *Anne*, whereof Mr. William Peirce was Mr and aboute a week or 10 days after came in the pinass. They brought 60. persons for the generall, some of them being very usefull persons, and became good members to the body, and some were wives and children of shuch as were hear allready. And some were so bad, as they were faine to be at charge to send them home againe the next year. Also besides these ther came a company that did belong to the generall body, but came on their perticuler, and were to have lands assigned them and be for themselves." This refers to John Oldham and his associates, ten in number.

Robert Cushman had written to Bradford early that year: "Our friends at Leyden . . . will come to you as many as can this time," and by the ship *Anne* he sent another letter, advising Bradford that "Some few of your old friends are come, as &c. So they come droping to you. . . . And because people press so hard upon us to goe, and often shuch as are none of the fitest, I pray you write earnestly to the Treasurer and direct what persons should be sente. It greeveth me to see so weake a company sent you, and yet had I not been hear they had been weaker. . . . Shuch and shuch came without my consente: but the importunitie of their freinds got promise of our Treasurer in my absence."

From these statements can be learned the reason for the disappearance from Plymouth of many of the first arrivals after a few years' trial of the hardships of pioneer life. They were sent back by the officials as unfitted to the task of planting a colony in the wilderness.

ANTHONY ANNABLE

HE was from Cambridge (City), co. Cambridge, where he married Jane Momford, 26 April, 1619 *(Parish Register All Saints, Cambridge)*. He brought his wife and two children with him for which he drew four shares in the 1627 division.

Thomas Blossom, also from Cambridge, owning property in the parish of All Saints, became a member of the Leyden church and emigrated to Plymouth in 1629 with his wife, Anne Heilsdon, whom he married 10 November, 1605, at St. Clement's, Cambridge.

EDWARD BANGS

HE was a shipwright by occupation, baptized 28 October, 1591, at Panfield, co. Essex, son of John and Jane (Chavis) Bangs of Panfield and Hempstead, who were married 30 January, 1586/7. He drew four shares in the 1627 division for himself, his wife, Lydia, and two sons, Jonathan and John. He had married Lydia, daughter of Robert and Margaret Hicks of Southwark, about 1612, and accompanied his mother-in-law and family on the voyage over to join his father-in-law, who had preceded him in the *Fortune*. He probably resided in Southwark for some years before emigrating.

ROBERT BARTLETT

HE was a cooper by occupation. As he married after 1627, Mary, daughter of Richard Warren, who as a young girl was a passenger in the same ship, it is suggested that he was from that section of London whence came so many of the Pilgrim emigrants, either St. Botolph without Aldgate, St. Leonard, Shoreditch or St. Mary, Whitechapel.

He died in 1676.

THOMAS CLARK

HE came as a young, unmarried man and was allotted one share in the 1627 division. He has been called mate of the *Mayflower* but this is an error as John Clark was the name of the officer in question. He is also supposed to have come from Saltash, Cornwall, from the fact that his property in Plymouth was known by that name, but an examination of the parish records of St. Stephens, Saltash, does not disclose his name.

CHRISTOPHER CONANT

HE was son of Richard and Agnes (Charles) Conant, baptized at East Budleigh, co. Devon, 13 June, 1588; he went to London, 1609, and after apprenticeship was admitted freeman of the Grocers' Company, 14 March, 1616. He lived in the parish of St. Lawrence Jewry, London, the church where his brother, Roger Conant, the emigrant of 1623 to Salem, was married. Although married, he came without his wife and received one share in the 1627 division. He was living in Massachusetts Bay in 1630, being a juryman in November of that year. Probably returned to England.

ANTHONY DIX

HE was a mariner by occupation. His name is listed in the 1627 division but the number of shares is not stated. In 1636 he was living in Salem engaged in trade on the Maine coast. In 1639 he was lost at sea.

JOHN FAUNCE

HE was, perhaps, from Purleigh, co. Essex, where a family of that unusual name was living before 1600 (*Arch. Essex, Book "Draper"*). A Jonas Faunce was in the tax list of Stow Maris, five miles from Purleigh, in 1623 *(P. R. O. 112/608D)*. He received one share in the 1627 division.

EDMOND FLOOD

NOTHING is known of this passenger beyond his allotment of one share in the 1627 division. He probably died or left the Colony.

GODBERT GODBERTSON

THIS person (whose name is frequently written Cuthbert Cuthbertson) was a hat maker from Leyden, Holland, where he had been in church communion with the Pilgrims before emigration *(Winslow)*. He married there, (1) Elizabeth Kendall, 1617, and (2) Mrs. Sarah (Allerton) Vincent-Priest, widow of Digory, 13 November, 1621. He brought two step-daughters with him, Mary and Sarah Priest, who married Phineas Pratt and John Combe, respectively.

TIMOTHY HATHERLEY

HE was a feltmaker, living in the parish of St. Olaves, Southwark. He married there 26 December, 1614, Alice Collard. He returned to England and was taxed in Southwark, 1628, but came again to Plymouth two years later. He was a native of Barnstaple, Devonshire. His son Nathaniel was baptized 16 July, 1618, at St. Olaves, Southwark.

WILLIAM HEARD

BEYOND the fact that he was allotted one share in the 1627 division there is no further record of this passenger and he probably died or left the Colony.

EDWARD HOLMAN

HE was given one share in the 1627 division and returned to England. Said to be identical with one of the same name who embarked 22 June, 1632, for New England and resided in Plymouth Colony. No information has been obtained as to his English origin.

It is quite probable that he was related to James Sherley, Treasurer of the Merchant Adventurers, whose mother was Mary Holman (*Visitation of London (1633), pp. 235-6*). She was from Godstone, co. Surrey.

MANASSEH KEMPTON

THIS passenger came from Colchester, co. Essex, where he was a member of an early dissenting congregation in that city. He removed to London and became affiliated with the Separatists under the leadership of Henry Jacob, about 1620 *(Gould MSS.).*

After the death of George Morton, who came in the *Little James,* Kempton married his widow, who was Juliana Carpenter, daughter of Alexander.

ROBERT LONG

IT is possible that he was from Leyden, as in the 1627 division he had shares of land assigned to him in the same diivsion with the Brewsters. No further record is available and he probably died early or left the Colony.

EXPERIENCE MITCHELL

THIS passenger was a son of Thomas Mitchell of Amsterdam and Leyden, who was born 1566 according to affidavit. This family probably originated in Cambridgeshire in the parish of Eltisley. Two other emigrants to New England came from that same parish. An Edward Mitchell was resident in that parish 1628, and as this was the name of the eldest son of Experience the clue seems a strong one.

Experience Mitchell was in London in the summer of 1620, living with the Southworths at Heneage House or in that neighborhood *(Bradford, History, fol. 43–45)*, although he may have had a temporary domicile nearby at Houndsditch, as both he and Thomas Southworth lived at a place called Houndsditch, in Duxbury, after arrival in Plymouth. A brother of Mitchell remained in Amsterdam and as late as 1662 Experience was in correspondence with his nephew there, as well as with a member of the May family, near relative of the first wife of Governor Bradford. Both of these families were from the same county, and possibly connected by an early marriage.

THOMAS MORTON, JR.

THIS passenger was probably related in some way to others of his name previously considered but the degree of relationship is not known. He received one share in the 1627 division but nothing further is known of him. He either died or left the Colony.

MRS. ELLEN NEWTON

THIS lady was sometimes called Elinor. As she died in 1681, aged 83, she was a young widow of 25 when she emigrated. John Newton and Helen, his wife, had a son Jeremy baptized 13 May, 1621, at St. Nicholas, Colchester, which was an early Puritan centre in Essex. A William Newton married Ellen Jacus, 8 January, 1603/4, at St. Botolph's without Aldgate, London, but this combination, right as to names, is too early in date. As she and Mrs. Bridget (Lee) Fuller, wife of Samuel and a fellow-passenger, were given adjacent lots it is possible that a relationship existed between them. It is stated that she was a daughter of Peter Worden, Sr., who died at Yarmouth, Mass., in 1638, but this is given with necessary reservation. It seems reasonable to suppose that she was related to one or more of the passengers, as young widows did not travel alone, as strangers, on such voyages in that day.

JOHN OLDHAM

HE was, perhaps, originally from the town of Derby, Derbyshire, and related to Lucretia, the wife of Jonathan Brewster. He brought some associates with him, and together they received ten shares in the 1627 division. He may be the John Ouldham, merchant of St. Stephens, Coleman Street, London, living there 1629, when he testified aged forty years, concerning goods shipped abroad. The registers of that parish, however, do not give any information about his family and he was probably only a temporary resident there. He was associated as partner with Richard Vines, formerly of London, in the Patent of Saco, Me., in 1629, and these two with Isaac Allerton were engaged in trade along the coast of Maine as associates.

The Leyden records contain the bethothal of a Margaret Oldham in 1611, probably some relative of John, or Lucretia Oldham, the second wife of Jonathan Brewster.

John Oldham brought with him his wife "and family," one of whom was his sister Lucretia, who married Jonathan Brewster the next year. It is not believed that he had any children, but in 1635 two boys named John and Thomas Oldham, aged 12 and 10 years respectively, came to New England and were probably the "2 little boys that were his kinsmen" who were with him when he was killed in 1636 by the Indians at Block Island *(Bradford I, p. 412).* Thomas married and left descendants.

CHRISTIAN PENN

THIS passenger is assumed to be a female but no connection with any other passenger is known. She received one share in the 1627 division. As the second wife of Francis Eaton *(q.v.)*, of the *Mayflower* bore this rare baptismal name it seems probable that she married him between 1627 and 1633.

JOSHUA PRATT

ALTHOUGH this is a fairly common surname in England, yet the name of this passenger has not been encountered throughout four years of research in English archives. Joshua Pratt was brother of Phineas Pratt, who came to New England the previous year in Weston's employ, and was a part of the unfortunate settlement at Wessagussett, now Weymouth *(4 Mass. Hist. Coll.* IV, *476–486; comp. Bradford, fol. 94)*. As Weston drew most of his men from London it is probable that these two brothers came from that city. Joshua and Phineas are names peculiar to the Puritan era, and would be found among the Separatists living in or near the Pilgrim quarter of London, already described.

A family of this name lived in Chesham, co. Bucks, 1610–36, the head of which was a Joshua, the only instance coming to the notice of the author.

JAMES RAND

THIS passenger received one acre of land in the division of 1623, but nothing more is heard of him. He either died or left the Colony. Possibly from St. George's parish, Southwark.

ROBERT RATLIFFE

HE was a native of Cheshire and drew two shares in the 1627 division, indicating the existence of a wife; but no further record is available and he probably died early or left the Colony.

NICHOLAS SNOW

HE is probably identical with the Nicholas, son of Nicholas Snow of Hoxton, Middlesex, baptized 25 January, 1599, at St. Leonard's, Shoreditch, London, the parish adjoining St. Mary's, Whitechapel, where Stephen Hopkins (whose daughter Constance became his wife), was married in 1618. It may be inferred that the emigration of the Hopkins family was the occasion of Nicholas Snow's following them to Plymouth.

(See Warren.)

MRS. ALICE SOUTHWORTH

SHE was the widow of Edward Southworth, daughter of Alexander Carpenter and sister of Julian Carpenter, the wife of George Morton *(q.v.)*. She was betrothed to Edward Southworth, say-weaver of Leyden, 7 May, 1613, by whom she had two sons, Constant, born 1615, and Thomas, 1617, who accompanied her on the voyage. She married Governor Bradford, about a month after arrival, on 14 August, 1623. The Southworths and Gov. Bradford had lived in Heneage House, Duke's Place, London, for about a year prior to the sailing of the *Mayflower*. It is probable that the Southworth family came from the vicinity of Fenton, co. Notts, near Sturton-le-Steeple, the home of Rev. John Robinson *(P. R. O. Exchequer, Dep. 43–44, Elizabeth Michaelmas No. 3)*.

Southworth families lived in various parishes in that section of England before the Pilgrim exodus.

(See Mitchell.)

FRANCIS SPRAGUE

THIS name does not occur in the Leyden Archives, and in addition to this it is of great rarity in England. Early settlers of the name emigrated from Dorset to New England but no other occurrence of it is known. It appears as Spragg and sometimes as Sprake, and such few instances of its occurrence are found in the counties of Devon and Somerset. As none of the passengers have been traced to the West Country it is probable that this emigrant was a transient resident in London whence most of this company came. As two daughters shared with him in the 1627 division and he had a son-in-law in 1644 it is probable that he was married and past middle life when he emigrated.

The occurrence of the name of Spragg at Knutsford, co. Chester, whence came other emigrants to New England, indicates a possible connection between him and Ratliffe and Hilton who preceded him in the *Fortune (q.v.)*.

THOMAS TILDEN

HE was probably originally from Tenterden, co. Kent, where he was baptized 1 May, 1593, and younger brother of Nathaniel Tilden who emigrated in 1635 to Scituate. Thomas had three shares in the 1627 division but he probably returned to England as there is no further record of his residence in Plymouth.

A third brother, Joseph, was a Citizen and Girdler of London who became one of the Merchant Adventurers that financed the voyage of the *Mayflower*. He died in 1642. Thomas, the emigrant, probably lived in London also and may be the Thomas Tilden of Stepney, silk weaver, who married there in 1620, perhaps a second wife. He formerly lived at Wye, co. Kent, but nothing further is known of him after his return.

STEPHEN TRACY

HE came directly from Leyden where he married Tryphosa Lee, 18 December, 1621, but was originally of Great Yarmouth, co. Norfolk, and a say-weaver by occupation. He was probably son of Stephen Tracy, a freeman of Yarmouth in 1606 and a mariner by occupation. He had three shares in the 1621 division but returned to England and settled at Great Yarmouth. He was living there in 1655 when he gave a power of attorney to John Winslow to divide his property here among his children who remained in New England.

RALPH WALLEN

HE is named in the 1627 division without indicating the number of shares, but it is known that he had a wife, Joyce, who sold his land in 1648, as he had died some years previously. Nothing is known of their English origin and the name disappeared from Plymouth Colony records.

PASSENGERS

OF THE

LITTLE JAMES

EMANUEL ALTHAM, *Captain*

JOHN BRIDGES, *Master*

1623

THE LITTLE JAMES

THIS was a small boat described by Bradford as "a fine new vessell of about 44. tunne, which the Company had built to stay in the Countrie." On the voyage across she was separated from her consort and did not arrive in Plymouth for a week or ten days after the *Anne.* In addition to this difficulty the crew became mutinous and caused the Captain and Colony officials great trouble after landing. She was sent to the Maine coast on a fishing expedition and while there was blown on the rocks, bilged and sank in deep water. Captain Bridges was lost in this disaster. The surviving crew refused to aid in floating her and on their return to England an Admiralty suit was instituted in consequence. She was floated later by other assistance and served the Colony as a fishing vessel.

There is no separate list of passengers by this pinnace as those who came in the two boats are grouped together in the official records when the division of land was made to them. The author, however, has been able to identify several as passengers of this little vessel and their names follow. It is possible that there were a few others but the boat was too small to accommodate many. She was three months and two days on the voyage from Land's End.

WILLIAM BRIDGES

THIS passenger, who later settled at Charlestown, Mass., was perhaps a brother or kinsman of the Captain of the *Little James*, and may have come in this vessel. It is certainly known that he was a son-in-law of John Oldham and in a petition he states that he came over with his father-in-law twenty-one years before (1644). He married Mary Oldham who died about 1646 and he died two years later, leaving sons, Peter and Samuel, and a daughter, Mary Knight (Wyman Charlestown, 125).

EDWARD BURCHER

PROBABLY from St. Saviour's, Southwark, where an Edward Burcher was taxed in 1620 *(P. R. O. Subsidy 186/407)*. George Burcher of London, mercer, in 1641 directed a payment to be made to Edward Burcher, then of Lynn *(Lechford Note Book 213)*. In a letter from the captain of the *Little James* to James Sherley, one of the Merchant Adventurers, he wrote: "Father Birrtcher and his wife wear as hartey as the youngest in the ship," indicating that he was beyond middle life *(P. R. O. Admiralty Court Rec. Misc. Bdle. No. 1142)*.

JOHN JENNEY

HE was a cooper by occupation and called a "brewer's man" from Norwich. As the land on which he lived in Plymouth was named Lakenham it is probable that he was a resident of that parish which is a suburb of Norwich although his name does not appear in the parish register. His wife, Sarah Carey, whom he married in 1613 in Leyden, was from Monk Soham, co. Suffolk, and on the voyage "was delivered of a child in the Ship a month before we cam a shore and both are well yet, God be praised" *(Letter of Capt. Bridges to James Sherley dated 7 September, 1623).* This same letter gives interesting particulars about her husband, who was the ship's cooper.

GEORGE MORTON

THE late Morton Dexter, a descendant, thought that this passenger was born in Harworth, co. Notts, a merchant by occupation. There were Mortons taxed in Bawtry, a near-by parish, in 1379 *(P. R. O. Subsidy 206/49)*. He married at Leyden 23 July, 1612, Julian, daughter of Alexander Carpenter. She was baptized 17 March, 1584, at St. James church, Bath, co. Somerset. Capt. Bridges calls him "George Morten" without a prefix of respect.

FEMALE PASSENGERS

OF THE
ANNE
AND THE
LITTLE JAMES

FEMALE PASSENGERS

THE following wives of passengers who had arrived in the previous ships came in these two vessels, *Anne* and *Little James*:

Mrs. Hester Cook
Mrs. ——— Flavel
Mrs. Bridget Fuller
Mrs. Sarah Godbertson
Mrs. ——— Hilton
Mrs. Margaret Hix
Mrs. Frances Palmer
Mrs. Elizabeth Warren

The following women came as passengers in the same two ships and married shortly after arrival:

Mary Becket married George Soule.
Patience Brewster married Thomas Prence.
Fear Brewster married Isaac Allerton.
Barbara ——— married Myles Standish.
Mrs. Alice Southworth (widow) married Gov. William Bradford.
Mary Warren married Robert Bartlett.
Elizabeth Warren married Richard Church.
Anne Warren married Thomas Little.
Sarah Warren married John Cook.
Abigail Warren married Anthony Snow.
Mary Priest married Phineas Pratt.

Sarah Priest married John Combe.
Lucretia Oldham married Jonathan Brewster.

Eight wives accompanied their husbands on these two ships, and twelve children were brought by their parents.

INDEX OF NAMES

Adams, 105
Alden, 7, 19, 27, 28
Allerton, 4, 11, 14, 29, 30, 60, 75, 87, 88, 145, 154, 177
Altham, 167
Annable, 135

Bangs, 119, 138
Barker, 99
Barthelmore, 20
Bartlett, 139, 177
Barton, 101
Bassett, 106, 123
Beachamp, 103
Beale, 107
Billington, 31, 129
Blossom, 137
Blunden, 74
Bompasse (see Bumpas), 110
Bothall, 73
Bradford, vii, 2, 4, 7, 8, 11, 15, 16, 21, 27, 29, 32, 33, 34, 37, 38, 40, 44, 49, 61, 69, 89, 91, 103, 131, 151, 161, 177
Brewster, 2, 3, 4, 11, 35, 36, 37, 38, 39, 44, 89, 91, 108, 154, 177
Bridges, 167, 169, 170, 172, 173
Briggs, 33, 109, 119
Britteridge, 14, 40, 88
Browne, 41, 117
Bucket (Becket), 81, 177
Bumpas, 60
Burcher, 171
Button, 42

Cannon, 111, 129
Carey, 172
Carman, 111, 129
Carpenter, 13, 56, 131, 149, 161, 173
Carter, 43

Carvanell, 123
Carver, 3, 4, 8, 11, 44, 61, 65, 96, 103
Chandler, 45
Charles, 141
Chavis, 138
Child, 17, 20
Chilton, 45, 130
Chingleton, 113
Church, 177
Clarke, 19, 46, 140
Collard, 146
Combe, 145, 177
Comyngs, 87
Conant, 141
Conner, 112
Cooke, 4, 47, 177
Cooper, 49, 86
Crackston, 50
Cushman, 12, 16, 61, 103, 113, 135
Cuthbertson, 145

Davidson, 36, 37
Davis, 29, 50
Deane, 114
Delano (de la Noye), 115
Dermer, 90
Dewsbury, 115
Dexter, vii, viii, 1, 2, 3, 11, 121, 173
Dix, 142
Doty, 51
Dunham, 58

Eaton, 52, 63, 156
England, 53
English, 53
Evans, 93

Faunce, 142
Fisher, 61
Flavel, 116, 124, 177

181

Fletcher, 54
Flood, 144
Ford, 104, 117
Fuller, 13, 42, 55, 56, 94, 131, 153, 177

Gardiner, 57
Godbertson (see Cuthbertson), 145, 177
Goodman, 58
Gorton, 14
Gresham, 33
Grey, 19

Hanson, 33
Harris, 22
Harton, 98
Hatherley, 146
Hayward, 116
Heale, 8, 19
Heard, 147
Heilsdon, 137
Heneage, 13, 14
Hicks (Hix), 109, 119, 138, 177
Hilton, 118, 162, 177
Holbeck, 59
Holman, 148
Hooke, 60, 78, 110
Hopkins, 11, 14, 51, 61, 62, 63, 64, 68, 79, 91, 106, 160
Howland, 65, 87
Hoyt, 56
Hubbard, 83
Hughes, 28

Jacob, 149
Jacus, 153
Jefferson, 21, 22
Jenney, 172
Jepson, 78
Jones, 17, 19, 20, 23, 28, 57

Kempton, 149

Lane, 105
Langmore, 66
Latham, 67
Leaver, 8
Lee, 56, 153, 164
Leggatt, 44

Lester, 68
Libby, 45
Little, 177
Long, 150
Lyford, 118

Mahieu, 48
Margesson, 69
Martin, 19, 60, 66, 70, 76, 78, 110
Masterson, 54, 69
May, 15, 34, 151
Minter, 44, 71
Mitchell, 15, 16, 40, 151, 161
Momford, 137
Moore, 20, 72, 88
Morden, 36
Morgan, 52, 120
Morton, vii, 13, 33, 56, 121, 149, 152, 161, 173
Mourt, 8, 61, 117
Mullins, 8, 28, 43, 44, 73, 74

Naunton, 38
Nelson, 45
Newton, 153
Nichols, 17
Nicolas, 122
Norfolk, Duke of, 13, 14
Norris, 29

Oldham, 108, 135, 154, 155, 170, 177
Oliver, 98

Palmer, 123, 177
Parker, 19
Peck, 39
Peirce, 133, 135
Penn, 156
Pitt, 116, 124
Playne, 29
Porter, 120
Powell, 39
Pratt, 145, 157, 177
Priest, 75, 145, 177
Prince (Prence), 14, 125, 177
Prower, 70, 76

Rand, 158
Ratcliffe, 159, 162
Rider, 113
Rigdale, 77

Ring, 114
Robinson, vii, 1, 2, 3, 37, 44, 48, 59, 161
Rogers, 60, 78, 110
Russell, 57

Sampson, 14, 49, 64, 79, 86
Sandys, 38
Scrobs, 36
Sheffield, 21, 22
Shirley, 16, 148, 172
Short, 17
Simonson, 126
Singleton, 113
Smith, 50, 83, 118
Snow, 93, 106, 160, 177
Soule, 80, 84, 177
Southworth, 12, 13, 14, 15, 16, 40, 61, 151, 161, 177
Spooner, 39
Sprague, 162
Stacie, 127
Standish, 11, 63, 81, 83, 177
Sterry, 84
Steward, 128
Story, 84
Stowe, 16
Summers, 62

Tench, 111, 129

Thompson, 85
Tilden, 163
Tilley, 4, 14, 49, 79, 86, 87, 88
Tinker, 89
Tracy, 123, 164
Trevor, 90
Turner, 91
Twitt, 19

Vincent, 75, 145
Vines, 154

Wallen, 165
Walthal, 68
Warren, 11, 92, 106, 139, 160, 177
Waryner, 51
Welles, 36
Wentworth, 37
Weston, 5, 14, 16, 17, 63, 72, 86, 103, 104, 157
White, 44, 59, 85, 94
Wilder, 96
Willett, 71
Williams, 97
Williamson, 19
Wilson, 78
Winslow, vii, 2, 11, 63, 80, 84, 98, 99, 105, 115, 126, 130, 164
Worden, 153
Wright, 131

INDEX OF PLACES

Amsterdam, 1, 151
Ashburton, Devon, 72
Austerfield, Yorks, 32, 33, 34, 42, 44, 121, 131

Bahamas, 67
Barham, Suffolk, 94
Barnstaple, Devon, 146
Bath, Somerset, 173
Battersea, Surrey, 110
Bawtry, Yorks, 35, 36, 173
Beaminster, Dorset, 95
Bentley-cum-Arksey, Yorks, 32, 33, 34, 35, 69
Bermondsey, Surrey, 109, 119
Bermuda, 61, 64
Bethnal Green (Stepney), 106
Biddenden, Kent, 48
Billerica, Essex, 41, 70, 76
Blewberry, Berks, 127
Bramfield, Suffolk, 30
Bredon, Worcester, 98
Bristol, 52, 63
Budleigh (East), Devon, 141
Burstead, Great, Essex, 41, 70

Cambridge, 137
Canfield Parva, Essex, 65
Canterbury, Kent, 45, 48, 113
Cape Cod, Mass., 18, 103
Chattisham, Suffolk, 99
Chelmsford, Essex, 76
Chesham, Bucks, 157
Chettisham, Cambridge, 99
Colchester, Essex, 50, 149, 153

Dartmouth, Devon, 12, 18
Delfts Haven, Holland, 18
Derby, 154

Doncaster, Yorks, 2, 34, 44, 91
Dorking, Surrey, 73, 74
Dover, N. H., 118
Droitwich, Worcester, 80, 98, 130
Duxbury, Mass., 67, 151

Eckington, Worcester, 80
Eltisley, Cambridge, 151

Fenton, Notts, 161

Gilston, Herts, 72
Gimmingham, Norfolk, 69
Godstone, Surrey, 148

Harwich, Essex, 19, 20, 28, 57
Harworth, Notts, 173
Hawkwell, Essex, 50
Hempstead, Essex, 138
Hockley, Essex, 70
Hoxton, Middlesex, 160

Ixworth, Suffolk, 68

Jordan's, Bucks, 22

Kempsey, Worcester, 80, 98
Kensington, Middlesex, 68

Lakenham, Norfolk, 172
Lechlade, Gloucester, 125
Leyden, vii, viii, 1, 2, 3, 7, 11, 12, 13, 15, 17, 25, 29, 34, 36, 39, 44, 45, 48, 50, 53, 54, 55, 58, 59, 69, 75, 78, 88, 91, 94, 97, 104, 108, 114, 123, 126, 131, 137, 145, 150, 151, 154, 161, 164, 173
Lezant, Cornwall, 75
Lincoln, 36, 37

London, viii, 3, 5, 8, 11, 12, 13, 15,
17, 18, 20, 21, 25, 29, 31, 34, 38,
39, 43, 49, 51, 56, 60, 61, 62, 64,
65, 66, 68, 72, 74, 75, 77, 79, 80,
84, 86, 104, 105, 110, 111, 116,
118, 120, 124, 129, 141, 157, 163,
171

(PLACES IN LONDON)
Aldgate, 12, 13, 14, 16, 61,
All Saints, Barking, 125
All Saints, Great, 75
All Saints, London Wail, 75
All Saints, Stayning, 31
Bevis Marks, 13
Blackfriars, 21
Blackwall, 17, 21
Burys Marks, 13
Drury Lane, 8
Duke's Place, 12, 13, 15, 40, 161
Heneage House, 12, 14, 15, 16, 40,
61, 151, 161
Houndsditch, 13, 151
St. Andrew Holborn, 110
St. Andrew Undershaft, 14, 29, 79, 87
St. Augustine, 75
St. Bartholomew the Great, 60, 78, 110
St. Botolph, Aldersgate, 81
St. Botolph, Aldgate, 14, 31, 65, 93, 105, 139, 153
St. Botolph, Billingsgate, 65
St. Bridget, 98
St. Catherine Coleman, 14
St. Dionis Backchurch, 29
St. Dunstan-in-the-West, 75
St. Giles, Cripplegate, 60
St. Giles in the Fields, 8
St. James Clerkenwell, 120
St. Katherine Cree, 14, 40
St. Lawrence Jewry, 141
St. Leonard's, Shoreditch, 14, 93, 139, 160
St. Margaret Patten, 75
St. Martin's in the Field, 47, 93
St. Martin's, Orgar, 51
St. Mary Aldermanbury, 68
St. Mary-le-Strand, 51
St. Mary Whitechapel, 14, 15, 61, 65, 91, 93, 106, 113, 123, 139, 160

St. Mary Woolchurch, 36
St. Mildred, Bread St., 29, 31
St. Mildred Poultry, 93
St. Peter, Cornhill, 68
St. Peter-ad-Vincula, 124
St. Stephens, Coleman St., 61, 154
St. Swithin, 65
Stepney, 20, 21, 104, 105, 106, 111, 123, 125, 163,
Wapping, 17

Monk Soham, Norfolk, 172

Neatishead, Norfolk, 89
Newbury, Berks, 29
Newport Pagnall, Essex, 65
New York, 71
Northwich, Chester, 118
Norton Folgate, Middlesex, 105
Norwich, Norfolk, 59, 71, 172

Ormskirk, Lancashire, 82

Panfield, Essex, 138
Plymouth (Eng.), 16, 18, 122
Plymouth, Mass., 5, 7, 15, 16, 20, 32, 34, 36, 45, 54, 62, 63, 67, 69, 71, 72, 91, 98
Prittlewell, Essex, 40, 50
Purleigh, Essex, 143

Ratcliffe (Stepney), 105, 125
Redenhall, Norfolk, 55, 56
Rolvenden, Kent, 113
Rotherhithe, Surrey, 20, 21

Saltash, Cornwall, 140
Sandwich, Kent, 45, 54, 78, 106, 113
Scrooby, Notts, 13, 15, 16, 35, 36, 37, 38, 39, 44
Shipton, Salop, 72, 86, 87
Shoebury (South), Essex, 40
Southampton, 16, 17, 18, 25, 27, 28, 55
Southwark, Surrey, 51, 104, 109, 114, 116, 117, 119, 138, 146, 153, 171
Stansill, Yorks, 32
Stoke, Surrey, 74
Stoke Bruern, Northants, 36

Stow Maris, Essex, 143
Sturton-le-Steeple, Notts, 44, 161
Sutton-cum-Lound, Notts, 36, 39

Tenterden, Kent, 163
Thurne, Norfolk, 89
Tickhill, Yorks, 32, 34, 89

Virginia, 38, 61, 62, 63, 68

Wakefield, Yorks, 34
Wellingly, Yorks, 32, 33, 34
Wilsyke, Yorks, 32
Wootton, Bedfordshire, 88
Worksop, Notts, 78
Wotton-sub-Edge, Gloucester, 63, 64
Wrington, Somerset, 56
Wye, Kent, 163

Yarmouth, Norfolk, 97, 164

www.ingramcontent.com/pod-product-compliance
Lightning Source LLC
Chambersburg PA
CBHW050633160426
43194CB00010B/1656